The Spelling Toolbox

Workbook 3

Linda Kita-Bradley

Grass Roots Press

Edmonton, Alberta, Canada

2004

The Spelling Toolbox – Workbook 3 is published by

Grass Roots Press

A division of Literacy Services of Canada Ltd.

PO Box 52192, Edmonton, Alberta T6G 2T5, Canada

PHONE	1-780-413-6491
FAX	1-780-413-6582
WEB	www.literacyservices.com

AUTHOR	Linda Kita-Bradley
CO-ORDINATOR	Pat Campbell
EDITOR	Judith Tomlinson
COVER DESIGN	Lara Minja – Lime Design
DESIGN	Patsy Price – Far Beyond Words
LAYOUT	Dish Design
PRINTING	Friesens

ACKNOWLEDGMENTS

The Word Origins were adapted from the following publication:

Hendrickson, R. (1997). *Words and phrase origins.* New York, NY: Checkmark Books.

We acknowledge the support of the Alberta Foundation for the Arts
for our publishing program.

Library and Archives Canada Cataloguing in Publication

Kita-Bradley, Linda, 1958-
          The spelling toolbox : workbook 3 / Linda Kita-Bradley.

ISBN 1-894593-31-6

          1. English language—Orthography and spelling. I. Title.

PE1145.2.K573 2004   428.1   C2004-904149-5

Printed in Canada

Contents

About this book

This spelling workbook aims to help adult beginner spellers develop a strategy-based approach to spelling. Although accurate spelling is the final goal, it is important that strategy building remain the focus as you and the learners work through the units in this book.

The first unit in the book introduces the five strategies, or spelling tools that the learners will use throughout the remaining twenty units. The five spelling tools are these:

- *Say, listen, and write.*
- *Find a spelling pattern.*
- *Divide and conquer.*
- *Use a spelling rule.*
- *Look for tricky parts.*

Units 2 to 21 begin with a theme-based word list followed by four parts.

■ Working with spelling tools

Learners do a series of spelling exercises that help them recognize how and when the five spelling tools can be used.

■ Trying out your spelling tools

Learners complete two dictations. The first dictation gives the learner a chance to spell the unit words as they appear in the unit word list. The second dictation manipulates the unit words in some way in order to give the learners an opportunity to choose any of the give spelling tools that can help them spell the new word. For example, if "sensible" is in the unit word list, then "sensitivite" or "sensitivity" may appear in the second dictation. Common sight words are also introduced in the second dictation.

■ Applying your spelling tools

After looking at an example, learners are asked to do a short piece of writing that relates to the unit theme. They are able to look at their spelling analytically and apply appropriate spelling tools while completing a real writing task.

■ A final word

Learners add spelling words to their personal spelling dictionary.

The workbook also includes the following:

■ Student glossary

The student glossary explains terms that the learner needs to know to complete the spelling exercises.

■ Word list

This list includes all the words that appear in the unit word lists. The list is presented alphabetically and indicates in which unit each word is found.

■ Notes for users

The notes primarily include complete dictations, word families, and explanations of the spelling rules introduced in the workbook.

■ Blackline masters

The spelling rules and word patterns can be photocopied for easy access and reference during lessons.

■ Feature: Word Origins

The origins of various words and sayings are presented throughout the workbook. Whether or not all these stories are completely true, it is hoped that you and the learners will find them both interesting and entertaining.

unit 1

introduction

Spelling Tools

You are going to use five spelling tools
to help you spell long words.

If you use the spelling tools in this book,
you will have a good chance
of spelling new words right...

and you will *remember* how to spell the words, too.

tool 1
Say, listen, and write.

Look at the words on the following page.
They are divided into parts.

Say each part of the word slowly.
Listen to each part.
Write each part as you say it.

Look at the words in the box.

re jec ted	_____
hos pi tal	_____
stu dent	_____

Which parts are easy to sound out and spell?
Which parts are hard to sound out and spell?

Sounding out parts of a word
is a good spelling tool to use.
But, if this spelling tool does not work,
try the next spelling tool.

tool 2
Find a spelling pattern.

A spelling pattern is a common group of letters.
For example, **tion** is a common spelling pattern.

Look at this group of words.
What is the common spelling pattern?
Circle it.

station
gumption
emotional

Write the spelling pattern
in the first column.
Say it out loud.
Write a new word that has the spelling pattern
in the second column.

Note
1

_____   _____

You will see many spelling patterns in this book.
Try to remember them.
They will help you spell many words.

But, if this spelling tool does not work, try the next spelling tool.

tool 3
Divide and conquer.

If you have a long word, divide it into parts.
Look at each part in the long word.

Do you see
- ❑ common beginning parts?
- ❑ common end parts?
- ❑ little words you know?

1 — Look at these words.
They all have common
beginning parts.

Divide each word.
Write each word in parts in the first column.
Cover the word.
Write the word again in the second column.

pre / view	pre view	preview
re / make	re make	remake
un / happy	un happy	unhappy
disbelieve		
rewind		
undo		
prepackage		

2 — Look at these words.
They all have common end parts.

Divide each word.
Write each word in parts in the first column.
Cover the word.
Write the word again in the second column.

teacher / **s**	teacher s	teachers
shift / **ed**	shift ed	shifted
danger / **ous**	danger ous	dangerous
regretful		
drinkable		
carrying		
helpful		

3 — Look at these words.
They all have little words in them.

Divide each word.
Write each word in parts in the first column.
Cover the word.
Write the word again in the second column.

break / fast	break fast	breakfast
after / noon	after noon	afternoon
holi / days	holi days	holidays
eggplant		
favourite		
damage		
donkey		

Dividing a word into parts
is a good spelling tool to use.
But, if this spelling tool does not work,
try the next spelling tool.

tool 4
Use a spelling rule.

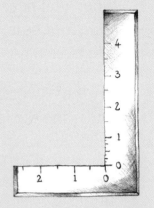

In this book, you are going to learn four spelling rules.

The four rules are
1. The *Doubling* rule
2. The *Y* rule
3. The *Silent E* rule
4. The *Drop the E* rule.

> **Tip**
>
> **These four spelling rules are on page 143 in this book.**
>
> **Make a copy of this page so you can check the rules when you need them.**

1 — The *Doubling* rule

If a word has ONE syllable and ends with ONE vowel and ONE consonant,
double the final consonant when you add an end part that starts with a vowel.

Say the base word.
Add the end part to the base word.
Say the new word.

Note 2

cram + ing _____

run + er _____

pen + y _____

strip + ing _____

flop + s _____

turn + ed _____

sleep + y _____

box + er* _____

bow + ing* _____

> ***x** and **w** are never doubled.**

2 — *Y* rule (part 1)

When you hear the **long e** sound at the end
of a word that has two or more syllables, use **y**.
You have a good chance of being right.

Say these words.
Underline the letter that makes the long **e** sound.

marry
salary
family
strawberry
dictionary

Now say these words.
Underline the long **e** sound in each word.

Note 3

everybody   mystery   readymade   bodyguard

Blow your own horn

In the 15th century, important people had trumpet
blowers walk in front of them. They did this so that
everyone knew important people were coming.
Common street sellers were too poor to pay trumpet
blowers, so they had to *blow their own horns*.

word origins

3 — The *Y* rule (part 2)

If a word ends in **consonant + y**,
the **y** changes to **i** when you add all end parts, except **ing**.

Say the base word.
Add the end part to the base word.
Say the new word.

picky + er   _____

marry + ed   _____

marry + age   _____

fussy + est   _____

mystery + ous   _____

study + ing   _____

hurry + ing   _____

family + s*   _____

play + er   _____

> *Change the **y** to **i** and add **es**. You always need to add **es** — not only **s** — so that the word sounds right. Compare **familis** and **families**.

4 — The *Silent E* rule

When you add the letter **e** to the end of a word,
the short vowel sound in that word changes to a long vowel sound.

Say the base word.
Add the letter **e**.
Say the new word.

not + e   _____

grip + e   _____

strip + e   _____

grim + e   _____

cop + e   _____

cloth + e   _____

bath + e   _____

scrap + e   _____

Now say these words.
Underline the part in each word
that follows the Silent E rule.

The first word is an example.

Note
4

<u>note</u>book	sideways	retirement
baseball	clothespin	flamethrower
snowflake	remakes	timekeeper

4— **The *Drop the E* rule**

If a word ends with a **silent e**,
     drop the **silent e** before you add
     an end part that starts with a vowel.

Say the base word.
Add the end part to the base word.
Say the new word.

Note
5

damage + ed   _____

lease + ing   _____

elevate + or   _____

base + ment   _____

smile + s   _____

surprise + ing _____

These four spelling rules will help you
spell many new words.

Now let's look at the last spelling tool.

tool 5
Look for tricky parts.

Some words have tricky parts.

Say the words in the box.
Each word has a tricky part.
The tricky part is marked.

Note 6

sneaky	You need two vowels to make the long **e** sound.
resign	The letter **g** is silent.
caught	The letters **aught** sound like **ot** in **hot**.
horrible	There are two **r's** in this word.
camera	The last part of the word doesn't sound clear.

How can you learn the tricky parts in a word?

Try these six steps. **Note 7**

1. **Say the word slowly.**
2. **Mark the tricky parts.**
3. **Study the tricky parts.**
4. **Cover the word.**
5. **Write the word.**
6. **Check the spelling.**

Bet your bottom dollar

Poker players put their chips or money in stacks. They take chips from the top of the stack to bet. If a player bets a whole stack or the last chip, he *bets his bottom dollar*.

word origins

1— Look at these words.
The tricky parts are marked.
Why are these parts tricky?

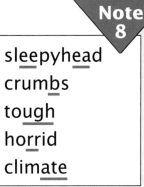

sleepyhead
crumbs
tough
horrid
climate

2— Look at the words again.
Look for the tricky parts.
Use the six steps to help you spell the tricky parts.

sleepyhead	_____
crumbs	_____
tough	_____
horrid	_____
climate	_____

**Now you are ready
to use your five spelling tools.**

Bootleg

Whiskey used to be illegal. Smugglers
used to hide whiskey in their tall boots.
The smugglers were called *bootleggers*.

unit
2

Leisure

Practice words

comedy	serious	horror
adventure	weird	mystery
favourite	thriller	hilarious

Working with spelling tools

Say, listen, and write.

Say each part of the word slowly.
Listen to each part.
Write each part as you say it.

com e dy	_____
thrill er	_____

Which parts are easy to sound out and spell?
Which parts are hard to sound out and spell?

With long words, some parts are easier
to sound out and spell than other parts.

Find a spelling pattern.

Look at these two groups of words.
What is the common spelling pattern in each group?
Circle it.

Note 9

adventure	serious
furniture	hilarious
picture	ridiculous

Write the two spelling patterns in the first column.
Say them out loud.
Write a new word that has the spelling pattern
in the second column.

_____	_____
_____	_____

Divide and conquer.

How can you divide
and conquer these words?

Divide each word.
Write each word in parts in the first column.
Cover the word.
Write the word again in the second column.

Divide and conquer.
Do you see
☐ **common beginning parts?**
☐ **common end parts?**
☐ **little words?**

favourite	_____	_____
horror	_____	_____
thriller	_____	_____
comedy	_____	_____

Use a spelling rule.

Say the base word.
Add the end part to the base word.
Say the new word.

Remember to check
your spelling rules.

Note 10

mystery + s _____

mystery + ous _____

comedy + s _____

comedy + ian _____

fame + ous _____

adventure + ous _____

adventure + s _____

Use a spelling rule:

Doubling rule

Y rule

Silent E rule

Drop the E rule

Look for tricky parts.

Look at the words below.
Look for the tricky parts.
Use the six steps
to help you spell the tricky parts.

Note 11

serious _____

hilarious _____

mystery _____

horror _____

weird _____

Remember to...

1. Say the word slowly.

2. Mark the tricky parts.

3. Study the tricky parts.

4. Cover the word.

5. Write the word.

6. Check the spelling.

Trying out your spelling tools

1— Listen to some sentences. Write the missing words.

Note 12

① That's my _____ _____.

② I love _____ _____ stories.

③ It's a really _____ _____.

④ It was a _____ _____.

⑤ I hate _____ movies.

2— Check your spelling.

Which words gave you trouble?
Use a different spelling tool. Try again.

3— Listen.
Write the new words and phrases.

This will give you a chance
to try out your spelling tools.

Note 13

Use your spelling tools.

Say, listen, and write.

Find a spelling pattern.

Divide and conquer.

Use a spelling rule.

Look for tricky parts.

① _____

② _____

③ _____

④ _____

⑤ _____

⑥ _____

⑦ _____

⑧ _____

4— Check your spelling.

Which words gave you trouble?
Use a different spelling tool. Try again.

Applying your spelling tools

1— Look at this example.

Here's a form from a video store.
What kinds of movies
does this person like?

RENT-ALL VIDEO STORE

List your favourite movies.

The Nutty Professor
Home Alone
Blazing Saddles

2— Your turn.

Fill out this form for your local video store.

RENT-ALL VIDEO STORE

How many movies do you watch a week?

Movies on TV: _____

Videos: _____

What kinds of movies do you like?

_____

_____

List your favourite movies.

_____

_____

THANK YOU.

A final word

Which words about **leisure** and **movies**
would you like to add to your dictionary?

Practice words

generous	pictures	appreciate
pleasure	congratulations	favour
certificate	fantastic	hospitality

Working with spelling tools

Say, listen, and write.

Say each part of the word slowly.
Listen to each part.
Write each part as you say it.

fan tas tic	_____
hos pi tal i ty	_____

Which parts are easy to sound out and spell?
Which parts are hard to sound out and spell?

With long words, some parts are easier
to sound out and spell than other parts.

Find a spelling pattern.

Look at these three groups of words.
What is the common spelling pattern in each group?
Circle it.

congratulations	fantastic	hospitality
relation	romantic	community
action	horrific	university

▼ Note 14

Write the three spelling patterns in the first column.
Say them out loud.
Write a new word that has the spelling pattern
in the second column.

```
_____    _____
_____    _____
_____    _____
```

Now look at these words.
Say them out loud.
Circle the spelling patterns you already know.

mention	future	generous	romantic
promotion	pictures	hilarious	reality
appreciation	features	realistic	community
congratulations	famous	terrific	university

Divide and conquer.

How can you divide
and conquer these words?

Divide each word.
Write each word in parts in the first column.
Cover the word.
Write the word again in the second column.

favour _____   _____

appreciate _____   _____

Use a spelling rule.

Say the base word.
Add the end part to the base word.
Say the new word.

Remember to check your spelling rules.

please + ing   _____

please + ant   _____

please + ure   _____

pleasure + s   _____

picture + s   _____

picture + ed   _____

picture + ing   _____

certificate + s   _____

certificate + ion   _____

appreciate + ed   _____

appreciate + ion   _____

Look for tricky parts.

Look at the words below.
Look for the tricky parts.
Use the six steps
to help you spell the tricky parts.

Note 15

generous _____

certificate _____

pleasure _____

congratulations_____

appreciate _____

Remember to...

1. **Say the word slowly.**

2. **Mark the tricky parts.**

3. **Study the tricky parts.**

4. **Cover the word.**

5. **Write the word.**

6. **Check the spelling.**

Break a leg

Stage actors are very superstitious.
They believe if you wish them good
luck, they'll have bad luck. So if you
wish them bad luck, they believe
they'll have good luck. That's why
you should say *"Break a leg"* to a
stage actor before he goes on stage.

· word origins ·

Trying out your spelling tools

1 — Listen to some sentences. Write the missing words. **Note 16**

① I sent you some wedding _____.

② I (appreciate) your _____ offer.

③ Can you do me a _____?

④ My _____.

⑤ _____!

⑥ What a _____ gift _____!

⑦ Thank you for your _____.

2 — Check your spelling.

Which words gave you trouble?
Use a different spelling tool. Try again.

3 — Listen.
Write the new words and phrases.

This will give you a chance
to try out your spelling tools. **Note 17**

Use your spelling tools.

Say, listen, and write.

Find a spelling pattern.

Divide and conquer.

Use a spelling rule.

Look for tricky parts.

① _____

② _____

③ _____

④ _____

⑤ _____

⑥ _____

⑦ _____

⑧ _____

4 — Check your spelling.

Which words gave you trouble?
Use a different spelling tool. Try again.

Applying your spelling tools

1 —   Here's a neat gift idea.

Gift Certificate

Congratulations, Sis!

I'm looking forward to seeing my new baby niece! Here's a gift certificate – 24 hours of free babysitting whenever you need it!

Love,
Jenny

2 —   Your turn.

Write a thank-you note for the gift in #1.

A final word

Which words about **family times** would you like to add to your dictionary?

unit 4

home

Shopping

Practice words

ketchup	lotion	scotch tape
deodorant	toothpaste	conditioner
razors	garbage	bandages

Working with spelling tools

Say, listen, and write.

Say each part of the word slowly.
Listen to each part.
Write each part as you say it.

ra zors	_____
tooth paste	_____
de o dor ant	_____

Which parts are easy to sound out and spell?
Which parts are hard to sound out and spell?

With long words, some parts are easier
to sound out and spell than other parts

Find a spelling pattern.

Look at these five pairs of words.
What is the common spelling pattern in each pair?
Circle it.

ketchup	scotch	kitchen
sketches	botch up	hitchhike

crutch	hatch
Dutch	scratching

Write the five spelling patterns in the first column.
The first one is an example.
Say the spelling patterns out loud.
What sound does the vowel make? Long or short?

Write a new word that has the spelling pattern
in the second column.

Note 18

etch	fetch

Look at this group of words.
What is the common spelling pattern?
Circle it.

| garbage | bandage | marriage |

Write the spelling pattern in the first column.
Say it out loud.
Write a new word that has the spelling pattern
in the second column.

| _____ | _____ |

Now look at these words.
Say them out loud.
Circle the spelling patterns you already know.

conditioner	fixtures	scotch tape
lotion	generic	bandage
dentures	ketchup	package

 ## Divide and conquer.

How can you divide
and conquer these words?

Divide each word.
Write each word in parts in the first column.
Cover the word.
Write the word again in the second column.

Divide and conquer.

Do you see

☐ **common beginning parts?**

☐ **common end parts?**

☐ **little words?**

ketchup	_____	_____
toothpaste	_____	_____
garbage	_____	_____
bandages	_____	_____
razors	_____	_____

Use a spelling rule.

Say the base word.
Add the end part to the base word.
Say the new word

Remember to check your spelling rules.

tape + ed   _____

tape + ing   _____

tape + s   _____

bandage + s   _____

bandage + ing _____

Use a spelling rule:

Doubling rule
Y rule
Silent E rule
Drop the E rule

Look for tricky parts.

Look at the words below.
Look for the tricky parts.
Use the six steps
to help you spell the tricky parts.

deodorant   _____

razors   _____

conditioner _____

lotion   _____

Remember to...

1. Say the word slowly.

2. Mark the tricky parts.

3. Study the tricky parts.

4. Cover the word.

5. Write the word.

6. Check the spelling.

Trying out your spelling tools

1 — Listen to the shopping list. Write the missing words.

Note 19

① _____ , _____ and _____ .

② hand _____ and _____ .

③ _____ bags.

④ _____ _____ and _____ .

⑤ shampoo and _____ .

2 — Check your spelling.

Which words gave you trouble?
Use a different spelling tool. Try again.

3 — Listen to another shopping list.

This will give you a chance
to try out your spelling tools.

Note 20

> ### Use your spelling tools.
>
> **Say, listen, and write.**
>
> **Find a spelling pattern.**
>
> **Divide and conquer.**
>
> **Use a spelling rule.**
>
> **Look for tricky parts.**

① _____

② _____

③ _____

④ _____

⑤ _____

⑥ _____

⑦ _____

⑧ _____

Note 21

4 — Check your spelling.

Which words gave you trouble?
Use a different spelling tool.
Try again.

Applying your spelling tools

1— Look at the shopping list.

Which items
do you buy every month?

THINGS TO BUY

razor blades
mouthwash
deodorant
toilet paper
shoelaces
light bulbs
aspirin

Pharmacy supplies

baby aspirin

2— Your turn.

Look at the shopping list.
Add five things you need to
buy from the pharmacy section.

A final word

Which words about **shopping**
would you like to add to your dictionary?

Practice words

damaged	furniture	leakage
kitchen	cupboards	ceiling
furnished	electric	renovations

Working with spelling tools

Say, listen, and write.

Say each part of the word slowly.
Listen to each part.
Write each part as you say it.

dam age	_____
fur nish	_____

Which parts are easy to sound out and spell?
Which parts are hard to sound out and spell?

With long words, some parts are easier
to sound out and spell than other parts.

Find a spelling pattern.

Look at these words.
Say them out loud.
Circle the spelling patterns you already know.

renovations	furniture	electric	kitchen	damaged
condition	pictures	plastic	botched	leakage

Divide and conquer.

How can you divide
and conquer these words?

Divide each word.
Write each word in parts in the first column.
Cover the word.
Write the word again in the second column.

Divide and conquer.

Do you see

☐ **common beginning parts?**

☐ **common end parts?**

☐ **little words?**

furnished _____ _____

cupboards _____ _____

leakage _____ _____

Use a spelling rule.

Say the base word.
Add the end part to the base word.
Say the new word.

Remember to check your spelling rules.

Use a spelling rule:

Doubling rule
Y rule
Silent E rule
Drop the E rule

damage + s _____

damage + ed _____

damage + ing _____

renovate + s _____

renovate + ed _____

renovate + ing _____

renovate + ion _____

renovate + ion + s _____

Look for tricky parts.

Look at the words below.
Look for the tricky parts.
Use the six steps
to help you spell the tricky parts.

Note 22

kitchen _____

furnish _____

furniture _____

electric _____

leakage _____

ceiling _____

Remember to...

1. **Say the word slowly.**

2. **Mark the tricky parts.**

3. **Study the tricky parts.**

4. **Cover the word.**

5. **Write the word.**

6. **Check the spelling.**

Trying out your spelling tools

1— Listen to some sentences. Write the missing words.

Note 23

① There's water _____ on the bedroom _____.

② _____ never end.

③ There's weird _____ behind the _____
_____.

④ I need an _____ can opener.

⑤ It's _____ with used _____.

2— Check your spelling.

Which words gave you trouble?
Use a different spelling tool. Try again.

3— Listen.
Write the new words and phrases.

This will give you a chance
to try out your spelling tools.

Note 24

Use your spelling tools.

Say, listen, and write.

Find a spelling pattern.

Divide and conquer.

Use a spelling rule.

Look for tricky parts.

① _____
② _____
③ _____
④ _____
⑤ _____
⑥ _____
⑦ _____
⑧ _____

4— Check your spelling.

Which words gave you trouble?
Use a different spelling tool. Try again.

Applying your spelling tools

1— Read these business cards.

What trade is advertised?
Write the trade on the line.

PLUMBING Inc.

For all your plumbing needs.

TOILETS   PIPES   DRAINS

_____

WOODY'S WOOD REPAIR

stair repair
shelving
cabinets and cupboards

Woody's my name. Wood's my game.

_____

BEAUTIFUL YARDS

• planting and weeding •
• pruning and cutting •
• raking and watering •

For all your gardening needs!

_____

2— Your turn.

What needs to be fixed
in your home?
List three things.

_____

_____

_____

Look at your list above.
Who can fix these things?

_____

_____

_____

A final word

Which words about **fix it up**
would you like to add to your dictionary?

Chicken feed

North American settlers had lots of animals.
The big animals ate big pieces of grain, but
chickens ate small, broken pieces of grain
called *chicken feed*. Gamblers on riverboats
called small change *chicken feed*.

word origins

unit
6

home

Changes

Practice words

pressure	convenient	appliance
location	connection	condition
fridge	cancel	forward

Working with spelling tools

Say, listen and write.

Say each part of the word slowly.
Listen to each part.
Write each part as you say it.

cancel	_____
forward	_____

Which parts are easy to sound out and spell?
Which parts are hard to sound out and spell?

With long words, some parts are easier
to sound out and spell than other parts.

Find a spelling pattern.

Look at these five pairs of words.
What is the common spelling pattern in each pair?
Circle it.

badge	edge	midge	dodge	nudge
Madge	wedge	bridge	lodge	fudge

Note
25

Write the five spelling patterns in the first column.
The first one is an example.
Say the spelling patterns out loud.
What sound does the vowel make? Long or short?

Write a new word that has the spelling pattern
in the second column.

adge	badger
____	_____
____	_____
____	_____
____	_____

Look at these two groups of words.
What is the common spelling pattern in each group of words?
Circle it.

appliance
importance
maintenance

convenience
independence
science

Write the two spelling patterns in the first column.
Say them out loud.
Write a new word that has the spelling pattern
in the second column.

Note 26

——————— ———————————————

——————— ———————————————

Now look at these words.
Say them out loud.
Circle the spelling patterns you already know.

location	dangerous	distance
connection	hazardous	convenience
condition	electricity	maintenance
application	appliance	hodgepodge

Divide and conquer

How can you divide
and conquer these words?

Divide each word.
Write each word in parts in the first column.
Cover the word.
Write the word again in the second column.

Divide and conquer.

Do you see

 ☐ **common beginning parts?**

 ☐ **common end parts?**

 ☐ **little words?**

pressure ——————————————— ———————————————

connection ——————————————— ———————————————

cancel ——————————————— ———————————————

forward ——————————————— ———————————————

Use a spelling rule.

Say the base word.
Add the end part to the base word.
Say the new word.

Remember to check your spelling rules.

apply + ed	_____
apply + s	_____
apply + ance	_____
apply + ing	_____
pressure + ed	_____
locate + ed	_____
locate + ion	_____

Use a spelling rule:

Doubling rule
Y rule
Silent E rule
Drop the E rule

Look for tricky parts.

Look at the words below.
Look for the tricky parts.
Use the six steps
to help you spell the tricky parts.

Note 27

pressure	_____
convenient	_____
appliance	_____
condition	_____
cancel	_____
forward	_____

Remember to...

1. Say the word slowly.
2. Mark the tricky parts.
3. Study the tricky parts.
4. Cover the word.
5. Write the word.
6. Check the spelling.

Trying out your spelling tools

1— Listen to the list of things to do. Write the missing words. ▼**Note 28**

① Look for a _____ _____.

② Check water _____.

③ Check _____ of _____.

④ _____ cable _____.

⑤ _____ mail to new address.

⑥ Defrost _____.

2— Check your spelling.

Which words gave you trouble?
Use a different spelling tool. Try again.

3— Listen.
Write the new words and phrases.

This will give you a chance
to try out your spelling tools. ▼**Note 29**

*Use your
spelling tools.*

Say, listen, and write.

Find a spelling pattern.

Divide and conquer.

Use a spelling rule.

Look for tricky parts.

① _____
② _____
③ _____
④ _____
⑤ _____
⑥ _____
⑦ _____
⑧ _____

4— Check your spelling.

Which words gave you trouble?
Use a different spelling tool. Try again.

Applying your spelling tools

1— Read this ad.

If you wanted to
sublet this apartment,
what would you ask Bridget?

1-bedroom
apartment to sublet

AVAILABLE IMMEDIATELY

Convenient downtown location
(one block north of Main St. Bridge)

brand-new kitchen appliances
air-conditioning / balcony
fantastic city view

Call Bridget

2— Your turn.
You're looking for a new place.

Write an ad.
List what you want
in your new place.

Wanted Now! *A new place to live!*

Must have the following:

A final word

Which words about **home changes**
would you like to add to your dictionary?

unit
7

Practice words

support	programs	volunteer
donations	community	neighbours
hospice	services	involved

Working with spelling tools

Say, listen, and write.

Say each part of the word slowly.
Listen to each part.
Write each part as you say it.

sup port	_____
pro gram	_____

Which parts are easy to sound out and spell?
Which parts are hard to sound out and spell?

With long words, some parts are easier
to sound out and spell than other parts.

Find a spelling pattern.

Look at these words.
Say them out loud.
Circle the spelling patterns you already know.

donations	community	correspondence
communication	immunity	difference
quantity	advantage	judge

Divide and conquer.

How can you divide
and conquer these words?

Divide each word.
Write each word in parts in the first column.
Cover the word.
Write the word again in the second column.

Divide and conquer.

Do you see

☐ **common beginning parts?**

☐ **common end parts?**

☐ **little words?**

hospice _____ _____

service _____ _____

neighbour_____ _____

support _____ _____

Use a spelling rule.

Say the base word.
Add the end part to the base word.
Say the new word.

Remember to check your spelling rules.

commune + ity _____

community + s _____

donate + ion _____

donate + ed _____

hospice + s _____

service + s _____

involve + ed _____

Use a spelling rule:

Doubling rule
Y rule
Silent E rule
Drop the E rule

Look for tricky parts.

Look at the words below.
Look for the tricky parts.
Use the six steps
to help you spell the tricky parts.

Note 30

volunteer _____

neighbours _____

hospice _____

service _____

involve _____

community _____

Remember to...

1. Say the word slowly.

2. Mark the tricky parts.

3. Study the tricky parts.

4. Cover the word.

5. Write the word.

6. Check the spelling.

Trying out your spelling tools

1 — Listen to some sentences. Write the missing words.

Note 31

① Get _____ in _____ _____.

② _____ _____ need _____.

③ _____ your _____.

④ Do you know your _____?

2 — Check your spelling.

Which words gave you trouble?
Use a different spelling tool. Try again.

3 — Listen.
Write the new words and phrases.

This will give you a chance
to try out your spelling tools.

Note 32

Use your spelling tools.

Say, listen, and write.

Find a spelling pattern.

Divide and conquer.

Use a spelling rule.

Look for tricky parts.

① _____

② _____

③ _____

④ _____

⑤ _____

⑥ _____

⑦ _____

⑧ _____

4 — Check your spelling.

Which words gave you trouble?
Use a different spelling tool. Try again.

Applying your spelling tools

1 — Read this notice.

> # WANTED!
> # VOLUNTEERS!
> ### Drivers – Babysitters – Committee Members
>
> Support your BLOCK WATCH program!
> Donate your time.
> Donate money.
> ***It's to your advantage!***

2 — Your turn.

Reply to the notice above. How can you help?

> ## Support your BLOCK WATCH program!
>
> **How can you help?**
>
>   I can...
>
>   1. _____
>
>   2. _____

A final word

Which words about ***things to do*** in your community
would you like to add to your dictionary?

community

Action

Practice words

informed	suggest	decision
picket	organize	realize
advise	recommend	questions

Working with spelling tools

Say, listen, and write.

Say each part of the word slowly.
Listen to each part.
Write each part as you say it.

in form	_____
sug gest	_____
re com mend	_____

Which parts are easy to sound out and spell?
Which parts are hard to sound out and spell?

With long words, some parts are easier
to sound out and spell than other parts.

Find a spelling pattern.

Look at these five pairs of words.
What is the common spelling pattern in each pair?
Circle it.

Note
33

stack	checkers	sick	block	stuck
slacks	heckler	picket	shocking	mucky
backing	wreckage	tricks	pocket	chucked

Write the five spelling patterns in the first column.
The first one is an example.
Say the spelling patterns out loud.
What sound does the vowel make? Long or short?

Write a new word that has the spelling pattern
in the second column.

ack	cracker

Look at this group of words.
What is the common spelling pattern?
Circle it.

| decision |
| vision |
| collision |

Write the new spelling pattern here.
Say it out loud.
Write one new word
that has the spelling pattern.

Note
34

_____   _____

Now look at these words.
Say them out loud.
Circle the spelling patterns you already know.

options	relations	classic
questions	supervision	sewage
delegation	culture	picket

Divide and conquer.

How can you divide
and conquer these words?

Divide each word.
Write each word in parts in the first column.
Cover the word.
Write the word again in the second column.

informed	_____	_____
picket	_____	_____
organize	_____	_____
realize	_____	_____

Use a spelling rule.

Say the base word.
Add the end part to the base word.
Say the new word.

Remember to check your spelling rules.

decide + ed   _____

decide + ing   _____

decide + ion*   _____

realize + ed   _____

realize + ing   _____

realize + ation   _____

organize + ation   _____

advise + ing   _____

advise + ed   _____

Use a spelling rule:

Doubling rule
Y rule
Silent E rule
Drop the E rule

*When you add **ion** to words that have a final **d** sound, the **d** changes to **s**: **decide, decision** / **collide, collision** / **divide, division**.

Look for tricky parts.

Look at the words below.
Look for the tricky parts.
Use the six steps
to help you spell the tricky parts.

Note 35

picket   _____

advise   _____

decision   _____

question   _____

recommend   _____

organize   _____

realize   _____

Remember to...

1. **Say the word slowly.**

2. **Mark the tricky parts.**

3. **Study the tricky parts.**

4. **Cover the word.**

5. **Write the word.**

6. **Check the spelling.**

Trying out your spelling tools

1— Listen to some sentences. Write the missing words.

Note 36

① Should we _____ a _____ line?

② Make an _____ _____.

③ Can anyone _____ or _____ options?

④ _____ new members.

⑤ _____ anything is possible.

⑥ Any _____?

2— Check your spelling.

Which words gave you trouble?
Use a different spelling tool. Try again.

3— Listen.
Write the new words and phrases.

This will give you a chance
to try out your spelling tools.

Note 37

Use your spelling tools.

Say, listen, and write.

Find a spelling pattern.

Divide and conquer.

Use a spelling rule.

Look for tricky parts.

① _____

② _____

③ _____

④ _____

⑤ _____

⑥ _____

⑦ _____

⑧ _____

4— Check your spelling.

Which words gave you trouble?
Use a different spelling tool. Try again.

Applying your spelling tools

1— Here are the minutes
of a community meeting.

What are the concerns?

2— Your turn.

You get this form in the mail.
Fill it out.

Minutes of Meeting

Resolved: We need…
1. faster snow removal service.
2. garbage collection twice a week.

Action:
1. Advise community members.
2. Inform mayor.
3. Put pressure on council.

Monthly Community Meeting

Dear Community Member:
Flooding is a big problem
in our neighbourhood.
We need improved drainage.
Please suggest action to take.

Action:
1. _____
2. _____
3. _____

A final word

Which words about **community action**
would you like to add to your dictionary?

unit
9

Practice words

interested	positive	sciences
languages	general	international
courses	computer	special

Working with spelling tools

Say, listen, and write.

Say each part of the word slowly.
Listen to each part.
Write each part as you say it.

com pu ter	_____
in ter es ted	_____

Which parts are easy to sound out and spell?
Which parts are hard to sound out and spell?

With long words, some parts are easier
to sound out and spell than other parts.

 ## Find a spelling pattern.

Look at these two groups of words.
What is the common spelling pattern in each group?
Circle it.

positive	general
responsive	special
informative	international

Write the spelling pattern in the first column.
Say it out loud.
Write a new word that has the spelling pattern
in the second column.

Note
38

_____ _____

_____ _____

Now look at these words.
Say them out loud.
Circle the spelling patterns you already know.

international	basic	independence
qualifications	scientific	supportive
immigration	mathematics	special
future	language	national
curious	science	educational

Divide and conquer.

How can you divide
and conquer these words?

Divide each word.
Write each word in parts in the first column.
Cover the word.
Write the word again in the second column.

Divide and conquer.

Do you see

☐ **common beginning parts?**

☐ **common end parts?**

☐ **little words?**

interested _____ _____

international _____ _____

languages _____ _____

courses _____ _____

sciences _____ _____

Use a spelling rule.

Say the base word.
Add the end part to the base word.
Say the new word.

Remember to check your spelling rules.

language + s _____

compute + er _____

compute + s _____

compute + ation _____

compute + ing _____

science + s _____

Use a spelling rule:

Doubling rule
Y rule
Silent E rule
Drop the E rule

Look for tricky parts.

Look at the words below.
Look for the tricky parts.
Use the six steps
to help you spell the tricky parts.

interest _____

courses _____

general _____

special _____

science _____

language _____

Remember to...

1. **Say the word slowly.**

2. **Mark the tricky parts.**

3. **Study the tricky parts.**

4. **Cover the word.**

5. **Write the word.**

6. **Check the spelling.**

Fly off the handle

Axes were handmade in pioneer days. The axe head would get loose with use. Sometimes the axe head would fly off the handle of the axe. Now, *fly off the handle* means lose control or get angry.

word origins

Trying out your spelling tools

1— Listen to some sentences. Write the missing words.

Note 39

① They teach _____ at the _____ Centre.

② The YMCA offers _____ interest _____.

③ The local college has _____ _____.

④ The Cultural Centre holds _____ programs for kids every weekend.

⑤ The church is _____ in starting a teen group.

⑥ They have a really _____ attitude.

2— Check your spelling.

Which words gave you trouble?
Use a different spelling tool. Try again.

3— Listen.
Write the new words and phrases.

This will give you a chance
to try out your spelling tools.

Note 40

Use your spelling tools.

Say, listen, and write.

Find a spelling pattern.

Divide and conquer.

Use a spelling rule.

Look for tricky parts.

① _____

② _____

③ _____

④ _____

⑤ _____

⑥ _____

⑦ _____

⑧ _____

4— Check your spelling.

Which words gave you trouble?
Use a different spelling tool. Try again.

Applying your spelling tools

1— Look at these courses.

They are being offered by different centres in your community.
Check the courses you're interested in.

- ☐ Caring for Elderly Parents
- ☐ Figuring Out Your Tax Forms
- ☐ Gardening for Beginners
- ☐ Immigration Policy
- ☐ Rental Agreements: Questions to Ask

Community Learning Centre
Suggestion Box

What courses can we offer you?

Educational Courses

_____

_____

General Interest Courses

_____

_____

2— Your turn.

Fill in this suggestion form.

A final word

Which words about **community relations** would you like to add to your dictionary?

Practice words

protect	affect	quality
commercial	residential	industrial
division	rezone	invasion

Working with spelling tools

Say, listen, and write.

Say each part of the word slowly.
Listen to each part.
Write each part as you say it.

pro tect	_____
af fect	_____

Which parts are easy to sound out and spell?
Which parts are hard to sound out and spell?

With long words, some parts are easier
to sound out and spell than other parts.

Find a spelling pattern.

Look at these words.
Say them out loud.
Circle the spelling patterns you already know.

affection	industrious	protective
protection	quality	decisive
reaction	postage	intrusive
division	importance	industrial
invasion	pledge	commercial
venture	knowledge	residential

Divide and conquer.

How can you divide
and conquer these words?

Divide each word.
Write each word in parts in the first column.
Cover the word.
Write the word again in the second column.

> ## Divide and conquer.
> **Do you see**
> - ☐ **common beginning parts?**
> - ☐ **common end parts?**
> - ☐ **little words?**

rezone _____   _____
residential _____   _____

Use a spelling rule.

Say the base word.
Add the end part to the base word.
Say the new word.

Remember to check your spelling rules.

Note 41

quality + s _____
industry + s _____
industry + al _____
commerce + ial* _____
divide + s _____
divide + ed _____
divide + ing _____
divide + ion _____
invade + ed _____
invade + ing _____
invade + ion _____
rezone + ing _____

Use a spelling rule:

Doubling rule
Y rule
Silent E rule
Drop the E rule

*You need to add **ial**, not just **al**, so the word sounds right. **Ti** and **ci** make the **sh**-sound.

Look for tricky parts.

Look at the words below.
Look for the tricky parts.
Use the six steps
to help you spell the tricky parts.

commercial _____
affect _____
residential _____
quality _____
protect _____
rezone _____
industrial _____

Remember to...

1. Say the word slowly.

2. Mark the tricky parts.

3. Study the tricky parts.

4. Cover the word.

5. Write the word.

6. Check the spelling.

Trying out your spelling tools

1 — Listen to some sentences. Write the missing words.

Note 42

① _____ the _____ of the air.

② It's an _____ of _____.

③ Do you live in a _____ or _____ zone?

④ They want to _____ the _____ area.

⑤ How will it _____ you?

⑥ The new zoning _____ is great.

2 — Check your spelling.

Which words gave you trouble?
Use a different spelling tool. Try again.

3 — Listen.
Write the new words and phrases.

This will give you a chance
to try out your spelling tools.

Note 43

Use your spelling tools.

Say, listen, and write.

Find a spelling pattern.

Divide and conquer.

Use a spelling rule.

Look for tricky parts.

① _____

② _____

③ _____

④ _____

⑤ _____

⑥ _____

⑦ _____

⑧ _____

4 — Check your spelling.

Which words gave you trouble?
Use a different spelling tool. Try again.

Applying your spelling tools

1— Here's a notice from your community newsletter.

What's the problem?
How does the writer feel?

The city wants to rezone our neighbourhood. This means an invasion of strip malls and fast food joints. Let's say "No way!" to this change. Join the rally at City Hall this Saturday!

Chew the fat

Years ago sailors had a hard life. Sometimes they were at sea for a long time and didn't have much food. They often had to eat a lot of tough salt pork. The sailors would grumble about the tough pork as they chewed. Now, *chewing the fat* means grumbling, or talking.

· word origins ·

2— Your turn.

You decide to join the rally suggested in #1.
Write a poster to carry in the rally.

A final word

Which words about **community changes**
would you like to add to your dictionary?

unit
11

work

Forms

Practice words

confident	dependable	reliable
excellent	capable	responsible
independent	sensible	brilliant

Working with spelling tools

 ### Say, listen, and write.

Say each part of the word slowly.
Listen to each part.
Write each part as you say it.

con fi dent	_____
de pend	_____
in de pen dent	_____

Which parts are easy to sound out and spell?
Which parts are hard to sound out and spell?

With long words, some parts are easier
to sound out and spell than other parts.

 # Find a spelling pattern.

Look at these four groups of words.
What is the common spelling pattern in each pair?
Circle it.

(A)	(B)	(C)	(D)
confident	confidence	brilliant	brilliance
excellent	excellence	important	importance
independent	independence	relevant	relevance

Write the four spelling patterns in the first column.
Say them out loud.
Write a new word that has the spelling pattern
in the second column.

Note 44

Look at the groups of words again.
How are groups A and B the same?
How are groups C and D the same?

Look at these two groups of words.
What is the common spelling pattern in each group?
Circle it.

reliable dependable capable	sensible responsible horrible

Write the two spelling patterns in the first column.
Say them out loud.
Write a new word that has the spelling pattern
in the second column.

Note 45

_____ _____
_____ _____

Now look at these words.
Say them out loud.
Circle the spelling patterns you already know.

good-natured	dependent	capable
terrific	convenient	reliable
reference	important	dependable
confident	brilliant	responsible
excellent	applicant	sensible

Get the sack

In old Roman times, workmen carried their tools
in sacks. If the boss didn't like your work, he
handed you your sack of tools and your pay.
You were finished. If you *got the sack*, you
knew you were fired.

• word origins •

Divide and conquer.

How can you divide
and conquer these words?

Divide each word.
Write each word in parts in the first column.
Cover the word.
Write the word again in the second column.

Divide and conquer.

Do you see

❑ **common beginning parts?**

❑ **common end parts?**

❑ **little words?**

reliable	_____	_____
dependable	_____	_____
capable	_____	_____
independent	_____	_____

Use a spelling rule.

Say the base word.
Add the end part to the base word.
Say the new word.

Remember to check your spelling rules.

Use a spelling rule:

Doubling rule
Y rule
Silent E rule
Drop the E rule

rely + able	_____
confide + ent	_____
confide + ence	_____
sense + ible	_____
sense + s	_____
sense + itive	_____
response + ible	_____
response + ive	_____

Look for tricky parts.

Look at the words below.
Look for the tricky parts.
Use the six steps
to help you spell the tricky parts.

excellent _____

brilliant _____

Taken to the cleaners

Sometimes poker players or gamblers cheat. They play as a group against one player who doesn't know what's happening. The unlucky player loses all his money or gets *cleaned out*. In other words, he gets *taken to the cleaners*.

word origins

Trying out your spelling tools

1— Listen to some sentences. Write the missing words.

Note 46

① He's _____ with numbers.

② She's _____ of _____ work.

③ She's _____ and _____.

④ He's a _____ decision-maker.

⑤ He was _____ for a lot of positive changes.

⑥ I'm _____ and _____.

2— Check your spelling.

Which words gave you trouble?
Use a different spelling tool. Try again.

3— Listen.
Write the new words and phrases.

This will give you a chance
to try out your spelling tools.

Note 47

Use your spelling tools.

Say, listen, and write.

Find a spelling pattern.

Divide and conquer.

Use a spelling rule.

Look for tricky parts.

① _____

② _____

③ _____

④ _____

⑤ _____

⑥ _____

⑦ _____

⑧ _____

4— Check your spelling.

Which words gave you trouble?
Use a different spelling tool. Try again.

Applying your spelling tools

1— Read this reference letter.

What else would you need to know about Clarence
before hiring him?

> Clarence has great people skills.
> He's responsible.
> He's capable of standing up for
> himself when necessary.
> I think he would be an
> excellent employee.

2— Your turn.

Your friend is applying for a job.
She asks you to write a reference letter.
Write some positive things about her.

> *Please provide a character reference for the applicant.*
> *(35 words or less)*
>
> _____
>
> _____
>
> _____
>
> _____
>
> _____
>
> _____
>
> _____
>
> _____

A final word

Which words about **work forms**
would you like to add to your dictionary?

unit
12

work

Routines

Practice words

emergency	ordinary	advance
regulations	appearance	vacation
appointment	necessary	routine

Working with spelling tools

Say, listen, and write.

Say each part of the word slowly.
Listen to each part.
Write each part as you say it.

or din ary	_____
ad vance	_____
ap point ment	_____

Which parts are easy to sound out and spell?
Which parts are hard to sound out and spell?

With long words, some parts are easier
to sound out and spell than other parts.

Find a spelling pattern.

Look at these two groups of words.
What is the common spelling pattern in each group?
Circle it.

Note 48

ordinary	appointment
necessary	apartment
secretary	placement

Write the two spelling patterns in the first column.
Say them out loud.
Write a new word that has the spelling pattern
in the second column.

_____	_____
_____	_____

Now look at these words.
Say them out loud.
Circle the spelling patterns you already know.

vacation	glitches	negative
regulations	appearance	confidential
signature	advance	dictionary
dangerous	emergency	necessary
hectic	restrictive	advancement

Divide and conquer.

How can you divide
and conquer these words?

Divide each word.
Write each word in parts in the first column.
Cover the word.
Write the word again in the second column.

appearance _____ _____

appointment _____ _____

Use a spelling rule.

Say the base word.
Add the end part to the base word.
Say the new word.

Remember to check your spelling rules.

Use a spelling rule:

Doubling rule
Y rule
Silent E rule
Drop the E rule

emergency + s _____

ordinary + ily _____

necessary + ily _____

regulate + s _____

regulate + ed _____

regulate + ing _____

regulate + or _____

regulate + ion _____

regulate + ion + s _____

vacate + s _____

vacate + ion _____

advance + ment _____

advance + ing _____

advance + s _____

Look for tricky parts.

Look at the words below.
Look for the tricky parts.
Use the six steps
to help you spell the tricky parts.

emergency _____

appearance _____

appointment _____

routine _____

necessary _____

Kangaroo

James Cook was an early English explorer who explored Australia. He saw some funny animals that could jump very far. He asked a native for the name of the jumping animal. The native answered, *Kangaroo*, which meant "I don't know" in his language. So today, we call those jumping animals *kangaroos* or "I don't knows."

word origins

Trying out your spelling tools

1— Listen to some sentences. Write the missing words.

Note 49

① It's _____ to make an _____ in _____.

② The _____ are _____.

③ His _____ will get him the promotion.

④ What is the normal office _____?

⑤ In case of an _____, stay calm.

⑥ How much paid _____ time do you get?

2— Check your spelling.

Which words gave you trouble?
Use a different spelling tool. Try again.

3— Listen.
Write the new words and phrases.

This will give you a chance
to try out your spelling tools.

Note 50

Use your spelling tools.

Say, listen, and write.

Find a spelling pattern.

Divide and conquer.

Use a spelling rule.

Look for tricky parts.

① _____

② _____

③ _____

④ _____

⑤ _____

⑥ _____

⑦ _____

⑧ _____

4— Check your spelling.

Which words gave you trouble?
Use a different spelling tool. Try again.

Applying your spelling tools

1— Read these work place regulations.

Would you like to work here?
Why?

> # New Regulations
>
> Vacation times are now flexible.
> Pay advances are available.
> Routine locker checks are abolished.
>
> *My door is always open.*
> *No appointment necessary.*
>
> *By order of the new management.*

In case of an emergency, _____
_____ .

In case of fire, _____
_____ .

Wear protective _____
_____ .

_____ .

_____ .

2— Your turn.

What are some common
work place regulations?
Finish these regulations.
Add two of your own.

A final word

Which words about **work routines**
would you like to add to your dictionary?

work

unit 13

Memo Board

Practice words

schedule	temporary	permanent
January	February	August
December	immediately	rotation

Working with spelling tools

Say, listen, and write.

Say each part of the word slowly.
Listen to each part.
Write each part as you say it.

temp or ary _____

Jan u ary _____

Which parts are easy to sound out and spell?
Which parts are hard to sound out and spell?

With long words, some parts are easier
to sound out and spell than other parts.

Find a spelling pattern.

Look at these words.
Say them out loud.
Circle the spelling patterns you already know.

rotation	permanent	available
vacation	checkups	temporary
regulations	effective	January
manage	annually	February

Divide and conquer.

How can you divide
and conquer these words?

Divide each word.
Write each word in parts in the first column.
Cover the word.
Write the word again in the second column.

Divide and conquer.

Do you see

☐ **common beginning parts?**

☐ **common end parts?**

☐ **little words?**

temporary	_____	_____
permanent	_____	_____
immediately	_____	_____

Use a spelling rule.

Say the base word.
Add the end part to the base word.
Say the new word.

Remember to check your spelling rules.

temporary + ly _____

schedule + ing _____

schedule + s _____

schedule + ed _____

rotate + s _____

rotate + ed _____

rotate + ion _____

immediate + ly _____

Use a spelling rule:

Doubling rule
Y rule
Silent E rule
Drop the E rule

Look for tricky parts.

Look at the words below.
Look for the tricky parts.
Use the six steps
to help you spell the tricky parts.

schedule _____

immediately _____

permanent _____

February _____

August _____

December _____

Remember to...

1. Say the word slowly.

2. Mark the tricky parts.

3. Study the tricky parts.

4. Cover the word.

5. Write the word.

6. Check the spelling.

Trying out your spelling tools

1— Listen to some sentences. Write the missing words.

Note
51

① The _____ _____ is now _____.

② The vacation times for _____ are still _____.

③ Sign up for _____ and _____ courses now!

④ The deadline is _____ 1st.

⑤ The new regulations come into effect _____.

2— Check your spelling.

Which words gave you trouble?
Use a different spelling tool. Try again.

3— Listen.
Write the new words and phrases.

This will give you a chance
to try out your spelling tools.

Note
52

> ### *Use your spelling tools.*
>
> **Say, listen, and write.**
>
> **Find a spelling pattern.**
>
> **Divide and conquer.**
>
> **Use a spelling rule.**
>
> **Look for tricky parts.**

① _____

② _____

③ _____

④ _____

⑤ _____

⑥ _____

⑦ _____

⑧ _____

4— Check your spelling.

Which words gave you trouble?
Use a different spelling tool. Try again.

Applying your spelling tools

1— Here is a notice on a memo board.

Who should read it?
Why is the notice important?

> **TO:**   All temporary staff
> **FROM:** Systems Department
>
> We are starting a new rotation of shifts.
> It is effective immediately.
> See your supervisor for new schedules.

Clam up

When clams are scared, they shut their shells tight. When you *clam up*, you shut your lips tight. *Clam up* means to be quiet and not talk.

word origins

2— Your turn.

Complete these notices for the memo board.
Use a word that makes sense.

Note
53

Memo 1

The new work schedule is effective _____ !

Memo 2

All _____
staff report to main office today.
The temp. agency representative is available for questions.

Memo 3

Check the updated vacation _____ .
Make sure your name appears somewhere.

Memo 4

The following months are still open.
Sign on the dotted line for courses.

1. November _____ ___ S. Sabah
2. _____ _____
3. _____ _____
4. _____ Yvonne Barrett
5. March _____

A final word

Which words about **memo board**
would you like to add to your dictionary?

work Relations

Practice words

supervisor	foreman	secretary
management	administration	department
personnel	assistant	accounts

Working with spelling tools

Say, listen, and write.

Say each part of the word slowly.
Listen to each part.
Write each part as you say it.

su per vis or	_____
per son nel	_____
de part ment	_____

The Spelling Toolbox ■ **Workbook 3**

Which parts are easy to sound out and spell?
Which parts are hard to sound out and spell?

With long words, some parts are easier
to sound out and spell than other parts.

Find a spelling pattern.

Look at these words.
Say them out loud.
Circle the spelling patterns you already know.

administration	assistant	compliment
satisfaction	administrative	complimentary
manage	punctual	management
grievance	secretary	department

Divide and conquer.

How can you divide
and conquer these words?

Divide each word.
Write each word in parts in the first column.
Cover the word.
Write the word again in the second column.

Divide and conquer.

Do you see

☐ **common beginning parts?**

☐ **common end parts?**

☐ **little words?**

supervisor	_____	_____
management	_____	_____
personnel	_____	_____
foreman	_____	_____
assistant	_____	_____
secretary	_____	_____
department	_____	_____
accounts	_____	_____

Use a spelling rule.

Say the base word.
Add the end part to the base word.
Say the new word.

Remember to check your spelling rules.

Use a spelling rule:

Doubling rule
Y rule
Silent E rule
Drop the E rule

secretary + s _____

secretary + al _____

supervise + or _____

supervise + ing _____

manage + er _____

manage + s _____

manage + ment _____

manage + ing _____

administrate + or _____

administrate + ion _____

administrate + ive _____

administrate + s _____

Look for tricky parts.

Look at the words below.
Look for the tricky parts.
Use the six steps
to help you spell the tricky parts.

Remember to...

1. **Say the word slowly.**

2. **Mark the tricky parts.**

3. **Study the tricky parts.**

4. **Cover the word.**

5. **Write the word.**

6. **Check the spelling.**

supervisor _____

personnel _____

foreman _____

assistant _____

accounts _____

Trying out your spelling tools

1— Listen to some sentences. Write the missing words.

Note 54

① The _____ _____ handles that.

② _____ made some changes.

③ The _____ and _____ have to go.

④ I'm an _____ in the _____ office.

⑤ Her _____ handles all the _____ details.

2— Check your spelling.

Which words gave you trouble?
Use a different spelling tool. Try again.

3— Listen.
Write the new words and phrases.

This will give you a chance
to try out your spelling tools.

Note 55

Use your spelling tools.

Say, listen, and write.

Find a spelling pattern.

Divide and conquer.

Use a spelling rule.

Look for tricky parts.

① _____

② _____

③ _____

④ _____

⑤ _____

⑥ _____

⑦ _____

⑧ _____

4— Check your spelling.

Which words gave you trouble?
Use a different spelling tool. Try again.

Applying your spelling tools

1— Read these memos.

Which departments should they go to?
Fill in the department name for each memo.

Memo 1

TO: _____
FROM: Sasha Wiggins
Re: Vacation Pay

My vacation pay does not add up.
Please check it.

Memo 2

TO: _____
FROM: Sasha Wiggins
Re: Sick Leave

I was docked 3 days for being sick.
But I handed in my medical note on time.
Please check your records.

Note 56

Memo 3

TO: _____
FROM: Sasha Wiggins
Re: Lunch room

The microwave and fridge are still not working.
Could somebody repair them, please.

$2-$ Your turn.

Write a memo for each situation.

a. You are moving to a new apartment.
   You need a copy of your pay slip.

Memo

TO: _____

FROM: _____

Re: _____

_____

_____

_____

---

b. You need to make a shift change.
   You find someone to switch with you.
   Write a memo that informs your foreman.

Memo

TO: _____

FROM: _____

Re: _____

_____

_____

_____

---

c. You found a new job.
    You have to give two weeks' notice.

Memo

TO: _____

FROM: _____

Re: _____

_____

_____

_____

A final word

Which words about **work relations**
would you like to add to your dictionary?

Breeze

There were a lot of Spanish sailors in the 16th century.
They called a wind *breza*. English sailors learned *breza*
from the Spanish and then changed *breza* to *breeze*.

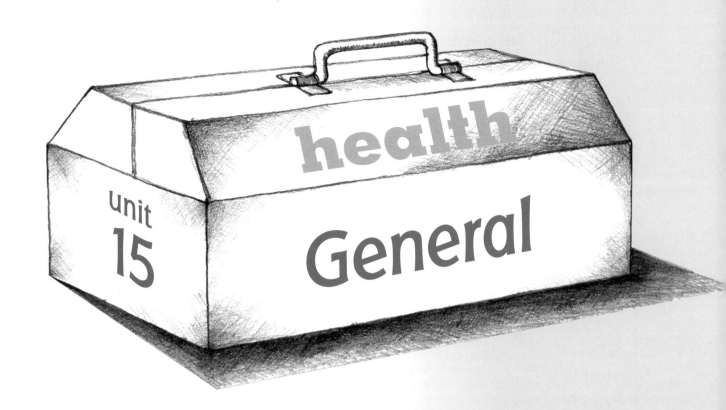

unit
15

health

General

Practice words

headaches	breathe	muscles
difficulty	dizzy	rough
cough	trouble	stomach

Working with spelling tools

Say, listen, and write.

Say each part of the word slowly.
Listen to each part.
Write each part as you say it.

dif fi cult _____

Which parts are easy to sound out and spell?
Which parts are hard to sound out and spell?

With long words, some parts are easier
to sound out and spell than other parts.

Find a spelling pattern.

Look at this group of words.
What is the common spelling pattern?
Circle it. **Note 57**

trouble
simple
crinkle
possible
muscle

Write the spelling pattern in the first column.

Write a new word that has the spelling pattern
in the second column.

_____ _____

Now look at these words.
Say them out loud.
Circle the spelling patterns you already know.

prescription	itchy	trouble
vision	scratches	muscle
rupture	crutches	handle
drastic	stitches	pimples

Divide and conquer.

How can you divide
and conquer these words?

Divide each word.
Write each word in parts in the first column.
Cover the word.
Write the word again in the second column.

headaches _____ _____

difficulty _____ _____

Use a spelling rule.

Say the base word.
Add the end part to the base word.
Say the new word.

Remember to check your spelling rules.

dizzy + ness _____

dizzy + ing _____

difficulty + s _____

ache + s _____

ache + ed _____

ache + ing _____

ache + y _____

breath + e _____

breathe + ing _____

trouble + ed _____

trouble + ing _____

trouble + s _____

Look for tricky parts

Look at the words below.
Look for the tricky parts.
Use the six steps
to help you spell the tricky parts.

headache _____

stomach _____

cough* _____

rough* _____

trouble _____

muscle _____

breathe _____

dizzy _____

Remember to...

1. **Say the word slowly.**
2. **Mark the tricky parts.**
3. **Study the tricky parts.**
4. **Cover the word.**
5. **Write the word.**
6. **Check the spelling.**

***Ough* is a common spelling pattern. It has many different pronunciations. Compare cough, enough, though, through, plough, and thought.**

Deadpan

In the 19th century, your face was called your *pan*. Poker players try to keep their face neutral. They don't like to show emotion. They try to have a *deadpan* face.

· word origins ·

Trying out your spelling tools

1 — Listen to some sentences. Write the missing words.

Note 58

① I have _____ with _____.

② My _____ still feels _____.

③ I'm _____ all the time.

④ All my _____ are really sore.

⑤ I have a bad _____ and can't _____.

⑥ I have _____ seeing things in the distance.

2 — Check your spelling.

Which words gave you trouble?
Use a different spelling tool. Try again.

3 — Listen.
Write the new words and phrases.

This will give you a chance
to try out your spelling tools.

Note 59

Use your spelling tools.

Say, listen, and write.

Find a spelling pattern.

Divide and conquer.

Use a spelling rule.

Look for tricky parts.

① _____

② _____

③ _____

④ _____

⑤ _____

⑥ _____

⑦ _____

⑧ _____

4 — Check your spelling.

Which words gave you trouble?
Use a different spelling tool. Try again.

Applying your spelling tools

1— Look at this medical form.

What might this patient have?

Patient Medical Report
Please tick your symptoms.

- ☑ dizziness
- ☑ vomiting
- ☐ fever and shivers
- ☐ achy joints

Others (please specify).

horrible headache
blurry vision
sensitivity to light

Note 60

Patient Medical Report
Please tick your symptoms.

- ☐ dizziness
- ☐ vomiting
- ☐ fever and shivers
- ☐ achy joints

Others (please specify).

_____

_____

_____

2— Your turn.

When was the last time
you were sick?
What were your symptoms?

Fill out this medical form.

A final word

Which words about *general health*
would you like to add to your dictionary?

Practice words

vegetables	simple	sprinkle
mixture	minute	combine
ingredients	simmer	recipe

Working with spelling tools

Say, listen, and write.

Say each part of the word slowly.
Listen to each part.
Write each part as you say it.

sim mer	_____
in gre di ent	_____

Which parts are easy to sound out and spell?
Which parts are hard to sound out and spell?

With long words, some parts are easier
to sound out and spell than other parts.

Find a spelling pattern.

Look at these words.
Say them out loud.
Circle the spelling patterns you already know.

mixture	chicken stock	ladle
delicious	occasionally	simple
cabbage	vegetables	sprinkle
ingredients	tablespoons	example
fudge	measurement	apple

Divide and conquer.

How can you divide
and conquer these words?

Divide each word.
Write each word in parts in the first column.
Cover the word.
Write the word again in the second column.

Divide and conquer.

Do you see

☐ **common beginning parts?**

☐ **common end parts?**

☐ **little words?**

vegetables	_____	_____
sprinkle	_____	_____
mixture	_____	_____

Use a spelling rule.

Say the base word.
Add the end part to the base word.
Say the new word.

Remember to check your spelling rules.

combine + s	_____
combine + ing	_____
combine + ation	_____
vegetable + s	_____
simple + y	_____
simple + ton	_____
minute + s	_____
simmer + ing	_____
sprinkle + ed	_____
sprinkle + ing	_____
sprinkle + er	_____

> ## Use a spelling rule:
>
> **Doubling** rule
> **Y** rule
> **Silent E** rule
> **Drop the E** rule

Look for tricky parts.

Look at the words below.
Look for the tricky parts.
Use the six steps
to help you spell the tricky parts.

vegetable	_____
minute	_____
recipe	_____
combine	_____
ingredient	_____

Remember to...

1. **Say the word slowly.**
2. **Mark the tricky parts.**
3. **Study the tricky parts.**
4. **Cover the word.**
5. **Write the word.**
6. **Check the spelling.**

Trying out your spelling tools

1 — Listen to some sentences. Write the missing words.

Note
61

① _____ the _____ in the sauce.

② This _____ _____ takes a _____
to prepare.

③ _____ the flour _____ with the eggs.

④ _____ chocolate shavings on the cheesecake.

⑤ The _____ are expensive.

2 — Check your spelling.

Which words gave you trouble?
Use a different spelling tool. Try again.

3 — Listen.
Write the new words and phrases.

This will give you a chance
to try out your spelling tools.

Note
62

Use your spelling tools.

Say, listen, and write.

Find a spelling pattern.

Divide and conquer.

Use a spelling rule.

Look for tricky parts.

① _____
② _____
③ _____
④ _____
⑤ _____
⑥ _____
⑦ _____
⑧ _____

4 — Check your spelling.

Which words gave you trouble?
Use a different spelling tool. Try again.

Applying your spelling tools

1 — Here's a simple recipe for vegetable stock.

Recipes: Vegetable Stock

Ingredients:
2 T. oil
2 onions, chopped
4 carrots, chopped
2 sticks celery, chopped
salt and pepper to taste

2.5 litres water
few fresh parsley sprigs
1 tsp. dried thyme
1 bay leaf
1 clove garlic

Preparation:
Heat oil in big saucepan. Cook onions until golden.
Add carrots and celery.
Saute for 4 minutes, stirring.
Add salt, pepper and 2 tablespoons of water.
Cover and cook for 5 minutes.

Add rest of water. Boil.
Add parsley, thyme, bay leaf, and garlic.
Reduce heat and simmer till all vegetables are tender.
Strain.

Easy street

If you have a lot of money, you don't have to work. You can walk up and down the street — all day! You're walking on easy street.

• word origins •

2— Your turn.

What is your favourite simple recipe?
Write it out on the recipe card.

Recipe: _____

Ingredients:

_____
_____
_____
_____
_____

Preparation:

_____
_____
_____
_____
_____
_____
_____
_____

A final word

Which words about **diet**
would you like to add to your dictionary?

Practice words

nervous	relaxation	restless
emotional	worried	distracted
depressed	normally	concentrate

Working with spelling tools

Say, listen, and write.

Say each part of the word slowly.
Listen to each part.
Write each part as you say it.

dis trac ted _____

Which parts are easy to sound out and spell?
Which parts are hard to sound out and spell?

With long words, some parts are easier
to sound out and spell than other parts.

Find a spelling pattern.

Look at these words.
Say them out loud.
Circle the spelling patterns you already know.

relaxation	crotchety	emotional
concentration	balanced	physical
nervous	relaxants	normal
anxious	depressants	mental
manic	talkative	irritable

Divide and conquer.

How can you divide
and conquer these words?

Divide each word.
Write each word in parts in the first column.
Cover the word.
Write the word again in the second column.

Divide and conquer.

Do you see

☐ **common beginning parts?**

☐ **common end parts?**

☐ **little words?**

emotional _____ _____
depressed _____ _____
relaxation _____ _____
normally _____ _____
restless _____ _____
distracted _____ _____

Use a spelling rule.

Say the base word.
Add the end part to the base word.
Say the new word.

Remember to check your spelling rules.

relax + s* _____

relax + ed _____

relax + ing _____

relax + ation _____

rest + ed _____

rest + ing _____

rest + less _____

worry + s _____

worry + ed _____

worry + ing _____

worry + some _____

nerve + ous _____

concentrate + ed _____

concentrate + ing _____

concentrate + ion _____

Use a spelling rule:

Doubling rule
Y rule
Silent E rule
Drop the E rule

*You need to add **es**, not just **s**.

This makes the words easier to say.

Add **es** to words that end in **sh**, **ch**, **s**, **x**, and **z**.

Examples: rushes, matches, buses, relaxes and buzzes.

Look for tricky parts.

Look at the words below.
Look for the tricky parts.
Use the six steps
to help you spell the tricky parts.

nervous _____

restless _____

concentrate _____

Remember to...

1. Say the word slowly.

2. Mark the tricky parts.

3. Study the tricky parts.

4. Cover the word.

5. Write the word.

6. Check the spelling.

Trying out your spelling tools

1— Listen to some sentences. Write the missing words.

Note 63

① I'm _____ and can't _____ today.

② I feel _____ today.

③ He's so _____.

④ I'm very _____ and _____ about my driving test.

⑤ Get some rest and _____.

⑥ I'm never _____.

⑦ He's (normally) outgoing and relaxed.

2— Check your spelling.

Which words gave you trouble?
Use a different spelling tool. Try again.

3— Listen.
Write the new words.

This will give you a chance
to try out your spelling tools.

Note 64

> ## Use your spelling tools.
>
> **Say, listen, and write.**
>
> **Find a spelling pattern.**
>
> **Divide and conquer.**
>
> **Use a spelling rule.**
>
> **Look for tricky parts.**

① _____

② _____

③ _____

④ _____

⑤ _____

⑥ _____

⑦ _____

⑧ _____

4— Check your spelling.

Which words gave you trouble?
Use a different spelling tool. Try again.

Applying your spelling tools

1— Here is a self-test from a magazine.

Is this person normal?

Are you a happy person?
Answer these questions and find out.

When you wake up in the morning, how do you feel?
☐ happy ☐ sad ☐ depressed ☑ other _ecstatic_

What is your general mood in the day?
☐ happy ☐ sad ☐ depressed ☑ other _blissful_

Do you have trouble falling asleep? ☑ yes ☐ no
If yes, why? _too happy to sleep,_
don't want to waste a minute of life!

How many times a day do you laugh?
☐ Never ☐ 0-5 times ☐ 5-10 times ☑ more _constantly_

2— Your turn.

What kind of person are you?
Write down five things that describe your character.

A final word

Which words about **mental fitness**
would you like to add to your dictionary?

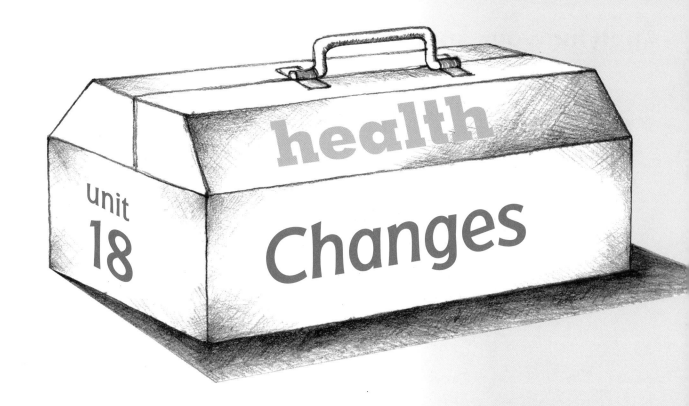

Practice words

forgetful	energetic	eighty
exhausted	guilty	elderly
mature	frustrated	active

Working with spelling tools

Say, listen, and write.

Say each part of the word slowly.
Listen to each part.
Write each part as you say it.

for get ful	_____
e ner ge tic	_____
frus tra ted	_____

Which parts are easy to sound out and spell?
Which parts are hard to sound out and spell?

With long words, some parts are easier
to sound out and spell than other parts.

Find a spelling pattern.

Look at these words.
Say them out loud.
Circle the spelling patterns you already know.

mature	realistic	dependent
dentures	activity	relatives
conscious	maturity	active
energetic	tolerant	feeble

Divide and conquer.

How can you divide
and conquer these words?

Divide each word.
Write each word in parts in the first column.
Cover the word.
Write the word again in the second column.

Divide and conquer.

Do you see

☐ **common beginning parts?**

☐ **common end parts?**

☐ **little words?**

forgetful	_____	_____
exhausted	_____	_____
guilty	_____	_____
eighty	_____	_____
elderly	_____	_____
active	_____	_____

Use a spelling rule.

Say the base word.
Add the end part to the base word.
Say the new word.

Remember to check your spelling rules.

frustrate + ed _____

frustrate + ing _____

frustrate + ion _____

mature + ity _____

active + ly _____

active + ity _____

active + ity + s _____

Look for tricky parts

Look at the words below.
Look for the tricky parts.
Use the six steps
to help you spell the tricky parts.

exhausted _____

mature _____

guilty _____

eighty _____

Remember to...

1. **Say the word slowly.**

2. **Mark the tricky parts.**

3. **Study the tricky parts.**

4. **Cover the word.**

5. **Write the word.**

6. **Check the spelling.**

Trying out your spelling tools

1— Listen to some sentences. Write the missing words.

Note 65

① My grandmother is a _____ _____ years old.

② She's _____ but _____.

③ The _____ are sometimes _____.

④ They can't be as _____ as they once were.

⑤ I feel _____ for not spending more time with her.

⑥ I'm usually _____ by the end of the day.

2— Check your spelling.

Which words gave you trouble?
Use a different spelling tool. Try again.

3— Listen.
Write the new words and phrases.

This will give you a chance
to try out your spelling tools.

Note 66

> ## Use your spelling tools.
>
> **Say, listen, and write.**
>
> **Find a spelling pattern.**
>
> **Divide and conquer.**
>
> **Use a spelling rule.**
>
> **Look for tricky parts.**

① _____

② _____

③ _____

④ _____

⑤ _____

⑥ _____

⑦ _____

⑧ _____

4— Check your spelling.

Which words gave you trouble?
Use a different spelling tool. Try again.

Applying your spelling tools

1— Here is a letter to an advice column.

What is the writer's problem?
What advice can you give?

> My mother is ninety years old.
> She's living with us now.
> She's great. But I feel so guilty.
> Looking after her is exhausting!
> I need a break. Any advice?
>
> Signed
> Guilty in Georgetown

2— Your turn.

Do you have elderly parents or relatives?
Who is responsible for their care?

What advice can you give people
who take care of the elderly?

1. Share the responsibility with other members of the family.
2. _____
3. _____
4. _____

A final word

Which words about *changes*
would you like to add to your dictionary?

unit
19

Lists

Practice words

earlier	exercise	watching
improve	excuses	choose
friendlier	expectations	attitude

Working with spelling tools

Say, listen, and write.

Say each part of the word slowly.
Listen to each part.
Write each part as you say it.

at ti tude _____

Which parts are easy to sound out and spell?
Which parts are hard to sound out and spell?

With long words, some parts are easier
to sound out and spell than other parts.

Find a spelling pattern.

Look at these words.
Say them out loud.
Circle the spelling patterns you already know.

resolutions	negative	disappointment
expectations	probable	improvements
exception	extraordinary	bundles

Divide and conquer.

How can you divide
and conquer these words?

Divide each word.
Write each word in parts in the first column.
Cover the word.
Write the word again in the second column.

Divide and conquer.

Do you see
- ☐ **common beginning parts?**
- ☐ **common end parts?**
- ☐ **little words?**

earlier	_____	_____
excuses	_____	_____
improve	_____	_____
friendlier	_____	_____
expectations	_____	_____
watching	_____	_____

Use a spelling rule.

Say the base word.
Add the end part to the base word.
Say the new word.

Remember to check your spelling rules.

watch + ing	_____
watch + s	_____
early + er	_____
friendly + er	_____
friendly + ness	_____
excuse + s	_____
excuse + ed	_____
exercise + s	_____
exercise + ing	_____
improve + ed	_____
improve + ing	_____
improve + ment	_____
choose + s	_____
choose + ing	_____
attitude + s	_____

Use a spelling rule:

Doubling rule
Y rule
Silent E rule
Drop the E rule

Gadget

The French word *gachette* means a little mechanical thing. The English changed *gachette* into *gadget*. Now, when you don't know the name of something, you can call it a *gadget*.

word origins

Look for tricky parts.

Look at the words below.
Look for the tricky parts.
Use the six steps
to help you spell the tricky parts.

early _____

improve _____

friend _____

exercise _____

watch _____

choose _____

attitude _____

Greenhorn

In pioneer days, oxen were used to plough fields. Young oxen were difficult to handle. They didn't know how to plough. Young oxen also have green horns. Now, anyone who is new at a job is a *greenhorn*.

word origins

Trying out your spelling tools

1— Listen to some sentences. Write the missing words. ▼ **Note 67**

① I have great _____ for next year!

② No more _____!

③ If you get up _____, you can _____.

④ He has to have a _____ _____.

⑤ I need to _____ my diet.

⑥ I want to stop _____ so much T.V.

⑦ _____ your friends carefully.

2— Check your spelling.

Which words gave you trouble?
Use a different spelling tool. Try again.

3— Listen.
Write the new words and phrases.

This will give you a chance
to try out your spelling tools. ▼ **Note 68**

Use your
spelling tools.

Say, listen, and write.

Find a spelling pattern.

Divide and conquer.

Use a spelling rule.

Look for tricky parts.

① _____

② _____

③ _____

④ _____

⑤ _____

⑥ _____

⑦ _____

⑧ _____

4— Check your spelling.

Which words gave you trouble?
Use a different spelling tool. Try again.

Applying your spelling tools

1— Look at this list of New Year's resolutions.

Which resolutions are realistic?

My New Year's resolutions

Improve my diet.
Get up earlier.
Exercise more.
Watch less T.V.
Learn a new language.
Paddle the Seven Seas.
Climb Mt. Everest.

2— Your turn.

Do you make New Year's resolutions?
Do you keep them?

List three resolutions you might keep.

A final word

Which words about *lists*
would you like to add to your dictionary?

Practice Words

believed	followed	laughed
realized	finished	dreamed*
decided	remembered	learned

*Also **dreamt.**

Working with spelling tools

Say, listen, and write.

Say each part of the word slowly.
Listen to each part.
Write each part as you say it.

fin ish	_____
re mem ber	_____

Which parts are easy to sound out and spell?
Which parts are hard to sound out and spell?

With long words, some parts are easier
to sound out and spell than other parts.

Find a spelling pattern.

Look at these words.
Say them out loud.
Circle the spelling patterns you already know.

questioned	experienced	flicked
recaptured	dodged	scribbled
scratched	edged over	fumbled
rummaged	wrecked	doodled

Divide and conquer.

How can you divide
and conquer these words?

Divide each word.
Write each word in parts in the first column.
Cover the word.
Write the word again in the second column.

Divide and conquer.

Do you see

☐ **common beginning parts?**

☐ **common end parts?**

☐ **little words?**

followed	_____	_____
finished	_____	_____
dreamed	_____	_____
laughed	_____	_____
remembered	_____	_____
learned	_____	_____

Use a spelling rule.

Say the base word.
Add the end part to the base word.
Say the new word.

Remember to check
your spelling rules.

Note 69

Use a spelling rule:

Doubling rule
Y rule
Silent E rule
Drop the E rule

follow* + ed _____

follow + ing _____

follow + s _____

dream + ed _____

dream + ing _____

learn + ed _____

laugh + ed _____

believe + ed _____

believe + abl _____

believe + ing _____

realize + ed _____

realize + ation _____

decide + ed _____

decide + ing _____

*You never double w.

Neck and neck

When two horses ran close together
in a horserace, people said they were
neck and neck. Now, in any close game,
we say the two sides are *neck and neck*.

· word origins ·

Look for tricky parts.

Look at the words below.
Look for the tricky parts.
Use the six steps
to help you spell the tricky parts.

Remember to...

1. Say the word slowly.

2. Mark the tricky parts.

3. Study the tricky parts.

4. Cover the word.

5. Write the word.

6. Check the spelling.

believe   _____

decide   _____

follow   _____

dream   _____

laugh   _____

learn   _____

Out of touch

Soldiers stay close together when they march. They stay so close together that their arms can touch the soldiers beside them. If the soldiers march badly, they get *out of touch*. Now, someone who is *out of touch* is confused or apart from a group.

word origins

Trying out your spelling tools

1— Listen to some sentences. Write the missing words.

Note 70

① I _____ my heart.

② I _____ his birthday too late, so I _____ to ignore it.

③ I _____ too late that I had _____ the wrong person.

④ They _____ when I said I've always _____ of a big wedding.

⑤ I _____ my lesson the hard way.

⑥ We _____ my birthday cake in record time.

2— Check your spelling.

Which words gave you trouble?
Use a different spelling tool. Try again.

3— Listen.
Write the new words.

This will give you a chance
to try out your spelling tools.

Note 71

*Use your
spelling tools.*

Say, listen, and write.

Find a spelling pattern.

Divide and conquer.

Use a spelling rule.

Look for tricky parts.

① _____

② _____

③ _____

④ _____

⑤ _____

⑥ _____

⑦ _____

⑧ _____

4— Check your spelling.

Which words gave you trouble?
Use a different spelling tool. Try again.

Applying your spelling tools

1— Read this diary entry.

> Dear Diary,
> Last night I
> dreamed I
> had a dog.
> The dog
> followed me
> everywhere.
> It really
> loved me.
>
> It even
> learned
> to fetch my
> slippers.
> When I woke
> up, I laughed.
> I don't even
> like dogs.

2— Your turn.

Think of a dream you had.
Write about it in your diary.

Dear Diary,

I dreamed

A final word

Which words about **Dear Diary**
would you like to add to your dictionary?

unit
21

Practice words

clinic	doctor's	graduation
practice	anniversary	holidays
payment	babysitter	due

Working with spelling tools

Say, listen, and write.

Say each part of the word slowly.
Listen to each part.
Write each part as you say it.

cli nic	_____
an ni ver sary	_____

Which parts are easy to sound out and spell?
Which parts are hard to sound out and spell?

With long words, some parts are easier
to sound out and spell than other parts.

Find a spelling pattern.

Look at these words.
Say them out loud.
Circle the spelling patterns you already know.

graduation	usual
vacation	anniversary
pick up	payment
check out	tournament

Divide and conquer.

How can you divide
and conquer these words?

Divide each word.
Write each word in parts in the first column.
Cover the word.
Write the word again in the second column.

Divide and conquer.

Do you see

☐ **common beginning parts?**

☐ **common end parts?**

☐ **little words?**

practice	_____	_____
payment	_____	_____
doctor's	_____	_____
babysitter	_____	_____
holidays	_____	_____

Use a spelling rule.

Say the base word.
Add the end part to the base word.
Say the new word.

Remember to check your spelling rules.

Use a spelling rule:

Doubling rule
Y rule
Silent E rule
Drop the E rule

holiday + s _____

anniversary + s _____

pay + ment _____

practice + s _____

practice + ing _____

graduate + ed _____

graduate + s _____

graduate + ion _____

Look for tricky parts.

Look at the words below.
Look for the tricky parts.
Use the six steps
to help you spell the tricky parts.

due _____

clinic _____

practice _____

doctor _____

anniversary _____

graduation _____

Remember to...

1. **Say the word slowly.**

2. **Mark the tricky parts.**

3. **Study the tricky parts.**

4. **Cover the word.**

5. **Write the word.**

6. **Check the spelling.**

Trying out your spelling tools

1— Listen to some sentences. Write the missing words.

Note 72

① The _____ opens at 10 a.m.

② The _____ _____ is _____ tomorrow.

③ My usual _____ is on _____ .

④ Our tenth _____ is next month.

⑤ My kid's _____ was yesterday.

⑥ Her baseball _____ starts at 6 p.m.

2— Check your spelling.

Which words gave you trouble?
Use a different spelling tool. Try again.

3— Listen.
Write the new words and phrases.

This will give you a chance
to try out your spelling tools.

Note 73

Use your spelling tools.

Say, listen, and write.

Find a spelling pattern.

Divide and conquer.

Use a spelling rule.

Look for tricky parts.

① _____

② _____

③ _____ ✻

④ _____

⑤ _____

⑥ _____

Note 74

⑦ _____

⑧ _____ ✻

4— Check your spelling.

Which words gave you trouble?
Use a different spelling tool. Try again.

Applying your spelling tools

1 — Look at the notes on this calendar.

What month might it be?

Note 75

			1	2	3	4
5	6	7	8	9	10	11
12	13	14 Clinic 2:30pm	15 Rent due	16 Norma's birthday	17	18
19 Shift change starts	20	21 Report cards 9:00 am	22	23 Phone new babysitter	24	25
26 Lori's track day 10:00 a.m.	27 Baseball tournament 1:00pm	28	29 School graduation 11:00am	30		

Rule of thumb

The last joint of your thumb is about 1 inch long. This is true for most adults. A long time ago, people used their thumb to measure things, but the measurement wasn't exact. Now, *rule of thumb* means a rough guide for something.

• word origins •

$2-$ Your turn.

Are you busy this month?
Fill in this calendar with your important dates.

			1	2	3	4
5	6	7	8	9	10	11
12	13	14	15	16	17	18
19	20	21	22	23	24	25
26	27	28	29	30		

A final word

Which words about **notes**
would you like to add to your dictionary?

Student Glossary

base word

A base word is a word that has no beginning parts and end parts.
Hat, **jump**, and **sun** are base words.
Hats, **jumped**, and **sunny** are not base words.

consonant

These letters are called consonants:
B C D F G H J K L M
N P Q R S T V W X Z
Sometimes **Y** is a consonant, too.

long vowel sounds

Long vowel sounds say their name.
The following words have long vowel sounds:
make Pete bike smoke cute

short vowel sounds

The following words have short vowel sounds:
tap pet sit pot hut

syllable

A syllable is a small part of a word.
Most of the time, a syllable has one vowel sound.
The following words all have two syllables:
Fri day bu sy say ing

vowel

The following letters are called vowels:
A E I O U
Sometimes **Y** is a vowel, too.

Word List

accounts (14)

active (18)

administration(14)

advance (12)

adventure (2)

advise (8)

affect (10)

anniversary (21)

appearance (12)

appliance (6)

appointment (12)

appreciate (3)

assistant (14)

attitude (19)

August (13)

babysitter (21)

bandages (4)

believed (20)

breathe (15)

brilliant (11)

cancel (6)

capable (11)

ceiling (5)

certificate (3)

choose (19)

clinic (21)

combine (16)

comedy (2)

commercial (10)

community (7)

computer (9)

concentrate (17)

condition (6)

conditioner (4)

confident (11)

congratulations (3)

connection (6)

convenient (6)

cough (15)

courses (9)

cupboards (5)

damaged (5)

December (13)

decided (20)

decision (8)

deodorant (4)

department (14)

dependable (11)

depressed (17)

difficulty (15)

distracted (17)

division (10)

dizzy (15)

doctor's (21)

donations (7)

dreamed (20)

due (21)

earlier (19)

eighty (18)

elderly (18)

electric(5)

emergency (12)

emotional (17)

energetic (18)

excellent (11)

excuses (19)

exercise (19)

exhausted (18)

expectations (19)

fantastic (3)

favour (3)

favourite (2)

February (13)

finished (20)

followed (20)

foreman (14)

forgetful (18)

forward (6)

fridge (6)

friendlier (19)

frustrated (18)

furnished (5)

furniture (5)

garbage (4)

general (9)

generous (3)

graduation (21)

guilty (18)

headaches (15)

hilarious (2)

holidays (21)

horror (2)

hospice (7)

hospitality (3)

immediately (13)

improve (19)

independent (11)

industrial (10)

informed (8)

ingredients (16)

interested (9)

international (9)

invasion (10)

involved (7)

January (13)

ketchup (4)

kitchen(5)

languages (9

laughed (20)

leakage (5)

learned (20)

location (6)

lotion (4)

management (14)

mature (18)

minute (16)

mixture (16)

muscles (15)

mystery (2)

necessary (12)

neighbours (7)

nervous (17)

normally (17)

ordinary (12)

organize (8)

payment (21)

permanent (13)

personnel (14)

picket (8)

pictures (3)

pleasure (3)

positive (9)

practice (21)

pressure (6)

programs (7)

protect (10)

quality (10)

questions (8)

razors (4)

realize (8)

realized (20)

recipe (16)

recommend (8)

regulations (12)

relaxation (17)

reliable (11)

remembered (20)

renovations (5)

residential (10)

responsible (11)

restless (17)

rezone (10)

rotation (13)

rough (15)

routine (12)

schedule (13)

sciences (9)

scotch tape (4)

secretary (14)

sensible (11)

serious (2)

services (7)

simmer (16)

simple (16)

special (9)

sprinkle (16)

stomach (15)

suggest (8)

supervisor (14)

support (7)

temporary (13)

thriller (2)

toothpaste (4)

trouble (15)

vacation (12)

vegetables (16)

volunteer (7)

watching (19)

weird (2)

worried (17)

Notes for Users

unit 1 • introduction • Spelling Tools

 Whenever you hear the suffix **shun**, it is spelled **tion**. When you hear the verb **shun**, as in "Don't shun me", it is spelled shun.

 You have to double the final consonant when you add an end part that starts with a vowel in order to save the short vowel's pronunciation. Compare **cramming** with **craming**, **runner** with **runer**, **stripping** with **striping**, and so on.

 The **Y** rule, part 1, works with compound words as well, as in **bodyguard**.

 The **Silent E** rule works in the middle of a word as well. Compare **notbook** with **notebook**, **basball** with **baseball**, and so on.

 The silent **e** is not dropped when adding end parts that start with consonants, in order to save the long vowel sound.

 In unstressed syllables, the vowel sound becomes shortened and often sounds like **uh** or **ih**. These unstressed syllables are more difficult to spell because the vowel sounds aren't clear or are lost completely, as in the word **camera** which is pronounced **camruh**.

 "Mark the tricky parts" means highlight the part by circling, underlining, highlighting with a marker, or separating off in some way.

"Study the tricky parts" means visualize the part in some way, spell it out loud, exaggerate the pronunciation, talk about how to remember it, etc.

 sleepyhead: double vowels making one sound; **crumbs**: silent **b**; **tough**: irregular spelling **ough** sounding like **uff**; horrible: double **r**; **climate**: second syllable unstressed making **ate** sound like **it**

unit 2 • home • Leisure

 Ture is never spelled **chur** in the middle or at the end of a word. (Compare with **church** and **churn**). **Ous** is a common ending for adjectives.

 It is important to say the new words because the stressed syllable changes sometimes when you add an ending. This can be helpful in two ways: (1) Unstressed syllables in base words become stressed in the new word. For example, note the stress change in the second syllable when you change **comedy** to **comedian**. If the word **comedian** is related to **comedy**, it is easier to remember that comedy is spelled with an *e*, not another vowel. (2) Thinking about the base words can help make sense of the spelling of longer words. For example, note the difference in the pronunciation of **please** when it becomes **pleasure**. It is easier to remember the *ea* vowel combination in **pleasure** if the word **pleasure** is related to **please**.

(In many cases, when two vowels go walking, the first one does the talking. In other words, when two vowels make one long vowel sound, it's the first vowel that is sounded, as in the words **please**, **rain**, **people**, and **boat**. This is a good pattern to remember because sometimes you know that a word has two vowels in it but cannot remember which vowel comes first. By saying the word, you know the vowel you hear comes first.)

 "I before E except after C" is a common spelling rule. There are some common exceptions: **weird**, **eight**, **height**, **weight**, **their**, **leisure**, **foreign**, **sleigh**, **neighbour**.

 Dictation
1. That's my (favourite) (comedy).
2. I love (serious) (adventure) stories.
3. It's a really (weird) (mystery).
4. It was a (hilarious) (thriller).
5. I hate (horror) movies.

 Dictation
1. comedies
2. scary mysteries
3. weird adventures
4. crazy thriller
5. fantasy
6. mysterious fantasies
7. captured by freaky things
8. natural powers

 Ic is a common ending for long adjectives (i.e., 2+ syllables). Compare **fantastic** with **sick**. Ity is a common noun ending.

 The consonants **C** and **G** are often soft when followed by the vowels *e*, *i* or *y* (**certificate** / **city** / **cycle** / **generous** / **ginger** / **gym**).

 Dictation
1. I sent you some wedding (pictures).
2. I (appreciate) your (generous) offer.
3. Can you do me a (favour)?
4. My (pleasure).
5. (Congratulations)!
6. What a (fantastic) gift (certificate)!
7. Thank you for your (hospitality).

 Dictation
1. short hospital stay
2. much appreciated
3. my favourite colour
4. congratulations on the promotion
5. generous hospitality
6. a romantic wedding day
7. a pleasant visit
8. sincerely yours

unit 4 • **home** • Shopping

 Short vowel + **tch** is a common spelling pattern.

Common exceptions are **rich**, **sandwich**, **which**, **much**, and **such**.

 Dictation
1. (toothpaste), (deodorant) and (razors)
2. hand (lotion) and (bandages)
3. (garbage) bags
4. (scotch) (tape) and (ketchup)
5. shampoo and (conditioner)

 Dictation
1. a head of cabbage
2. kitty litter
3. generic dishwashing soap
4. kitchen mitts
5. bags of groceries
6. butterscotch candies
7. wastepaper basket for bathroom
8. new juice pitcher

 G in **generic** and **c** in **groceries** are soft because of the **e**.

unit 5 • **home** • Fix It Up

 Ceiling is an example of the rule "I before E except after C."

 Dictation
1. There's water (damage) on the bedroom (ceiling).
2. (Renovations) never end.
3. There's weird (leakage) behind the (kitchen) (cupboards).
4. I need an (electric) can opener.
5. It's (furnished) with used (furniture).

 Dictation
1. electric bill
2. power shortage
3. good condition
4. a small glitch
5. damaged goods
6. plastic fixtures
7. picture frames
8. boarded up

unit 6 • **home** • changes

 Dge is used in these spelling patterns to maintain the short vowel sound in the word. Compare **bride** with **bridge**, **lode** with **lodge**.

 Note the difference in pronunciation of **ance** in **dance** and **appliance**. If ance is the stressed syllable, the short vowel **a** is clear (e.g. **dance**, **chance**, **romance**). However, if ance is not the stressed syllable, the short vowel **a** is reduced and sounds like uh or ih (e.g. **appliance**, **distance**). The same pattern follows for **ence**. Compare **hence** with **science** and **convenience**.

Because of the inconsistency in pronunciation, **ence/ance** are difficult spelling patterns. When in doubt of which to use, check with a dictionary.

 Some parts are tricky because the syllable isn't stressed, so the vowel sound is unclear. This is the case with the first syllable in **convenient**, **condition** and **appliance**, and **cel** in **cancel**.

Dictation
1. Look for a (convenient) (location).
2. Check water (pressure).
3. Check (condition) of (appliances).
4. (Cancel) cable (connection).
5. (Forward) mail to new address.
6. Defrost (fridge).

Dictation
1. forward the mail
2. application form
3. convenience stores
4. cancel newspaper
5. disconnect phone line
6. long distance calls
7. a botched up job
8. kitchen gadgets

unit 7 • community • Things to Do

(1) **Neighbour** is an exception to the "*i* before *e* except after *c* rule".
(2) Compare the pronunciation of *ice* in **nice** and **advice** with **hospice** and **service**. If *ice* is the stressed syllable, the *i* is long; if *ice* is not the stressed syllable, the *i* is short.

Dictation
1. Get (involved) in (volunteer) (programs).
2. (Hospice) (services) need (donations).
3. (Support) your (community).
4. Do you know your (neighbours)?

Dictation
1. community action
2. communities
3. free office space
4. support network
5. friends and neighbours
6. donate your time
7. involvement
8. advantageous

unit 8 • community • Action

Short vowel + *ck* is a common spelling pattern. Few common words (**trek**, **picnic**, **wok**, **yuk**) end in short vowel + *k* or + *c*.

Note the difference in pronunciation between **tion** and **sion**.

It is sometimes difficult to know whether to use *ize* or *ise*. **Ise** is more common in British spelling; *ize* in American spelling. **Advise** is always spelled using ise. **Organize** and **realize** can be spelled both ways. When in doubt, check with a dictionary.

Dictation
1. Should we (organize) a (picket) line?
2. Make an (informed) (decision).
3. Can anyone (recommend) or (suggest) options?
4. (Advise) new members.
5. (Realize) that anything is possible.
6. Any (questions)?

Dictation
1. volunteer organization
2. information meeting
3. decision-makers
4. solve the problem
5. suggestions and recommendations
6. backup plans
7. adult supervision
8. options and possibilities

unit 9 • community • Relations

 38 *Ive* and *al* are common adjective endings.

 39 **Dictation**
1. They teach (languages) at the (International) Centre.
2. The YMCA offers (general) interest (courses).
3. The local college has (computer) (sciences).
4. The Cultural Centre holds (special) programs for kids every weekend.
5. The church is (interested) in starting a teen group.
6. They have a really (positive) attitude.

 40 **Dictation**
1. general interest courses
2. optional courses
3. future programs
4. offer subjects in other languages
5. science projects
6. basic mathematics
7. a cultural difference
8. special qualifications
9. my specialty

unit 10 • community • Changes

 41 *Ti* and *ci* make the sh-**sound** when *al* is added to the base word, as in commer**cial** and residen**tial**. This spelling pattern also occurs when other endings starting with a vowel are added, as in spa**cious** and musi**cian**.

 42 **Dication**
1. (Protect) the (quality) of the air.
2. It's an (invasion) of privacy.
3. Do you live in a (residential) or (commercial) zone?
4. They want to (rezone) the (industrial) area.
5. How will it (affect) you?.
6. The new zoning (division) is great.

 43 **Dictation**
1. divide the property
2. intrusive regulation
3. an industrious person
4. commerce and industry
5. divide responsibility
6. pledge your support
7. change for equality
8. revision of the rules

unit 11 • work • Forms

 44 *Ent* becomes *ence*; *ant* becomes *ance*. When these spelling patterns are unstressed syllables, they sound similar. Because of this, it is sometimes difficult to know which to use. When in doubt about which to use, check with a dictionary.

45 *Able* and *ible* - like *ant / ance* and *ent / ence* – sound similar when they are unstressed syllables. When in doubt about which to use, check with a dictionary.

 46 **Dictation**
1. He's (brilliant) with numbers.
2. She's (capable) of (excellent) work.
3. She's (confident) and (independent).
4. He's a (sensible) decision-maker.
5. He was (responsible) for a lot of positive changes.
6. I'm (reliable) and (dependable).

Dictation

1. independent thinker
2. with confidence
3. a lot of capacity
4. so much responsibility
5. good-natured
6. a sensitive person
7. great sensitivity
8. sheer brilliance

unit 12 • work • Routines

 (1) Very few long words (i.e., 3+ syllables) end in **ery**. **Cemetery** is a common one that does. (2) **Ment** is a common noun ending.

 Dictation

1. It's (necessary) to make an (appointment) in (advance).
2. The (regulations) are (ordinary).
3. His (appearance) will get him the promotion.
4. What is the normal office (routine)?
5. In case of an (emergency), stay calm.
6. How much paid (vacation) time do you get?

 Dictation

1. quick advancement
2. ordinarily
3. appears confident
4. confidential papers
5. routine emergencies
6. responsibilities
7. necessary qualifications
8. using a dictionary

unit 13 • work • Memo Board

 Dictation

1. The (rotation) (schedule) is now (permanent).
2. The vacation times for (December) are still (temporary).
3. Sign up for (January) and (February) courses now!
4. The deadline is (August) 1st.
5. The new regulations come into effect (immediately).

 Dictation

1. suggestion boxes
2. regulate and rotate
3. time management
4. department head
5. available immediately
6. temporary layoff
7. temporarily locked
8. scheduling glitches

 Possible responses: Memo 1: immediately; as of now; today; as of tomorrow / Memo 2: temporary; part-time / Memo 3: schedule; roster; periods; times / Memo 4: December; January; February.

unit 14 • work • Relations

 Dictation

1. The (accounts) (department) handles that.
2. (Management) made some changes.
3. The (foreman) and (supervisor) have to go.
4. I'm an (assistant) in the (personnel) office.
5. Her (secretary) handles all the (administration) details.

Dictation

1. accounting department
2. all the foremen
3. departmental changes
4. assistant manager
5. supervisory team
6. ask for assistance
7. secretarial courses
8. administrative details

 Possible responses: Memo 1:
Accounting / Human Resources
/ Personnel; Memo 2: Human
Resources / Personnel; Memo 3:
Maintenance

unit 15 • health • General

 Consonant + *le* at the end of a word
is a common spelling pattern. The
le sounds like *ul*. In mu*scle*, the *sc*
combines with *le* to sound like *sul*.

 Dictation

1. I have (trouble) with
   (headaches).
2. My (stomach) still feels (rough).
3. I'm (dizzy) all the time.
4. All my (muscles) are really sore.
5. I have a bad (cough) and can't
   (breathe).
6. I have (difficulty) seeing things in
   the distance.

 Dictation

1. double trouble
2. stomach ache
3. achy joints
4. dizziness
5. a serious operation
6. a pimply rash
7. itchiness and rashes
8. out of breath

 Possible response: migraine
headache

unit 16 • health • Diet

 Dictation

1. (Simmer) the (vegetables) in the
   sauce.
2. This (simple) (recipe) takes a
   (minute) to prepare.
3. (Combine) the flour (mixture)
   with the eggs.
4. (Sprinkle) chocolate shavings on
   the cheesecake.
5. The (ingredients) are expensive.

 Dictation

1. saucepan
2. cookbooks
3. cake mix
4. pancake mixes
5. white sauce
6. batches of cookies
7. vegetable stock
8. coconut sprinkles

unit 17 • health • Fitness

 Dictation

1. I'm (distracted) and can't
   (concentrate) today.
2. I feel (restless) today.
3. He's so (emotional).
4. I'm very (nervous) and (worried)
   about my driving test.
5. Get some rest and (relaxation).
6. I'm never (depressed).
7. He's (normally) outgoing and
   relaxed.

 Dictation

1. talkative
2. lack concentration
3. usually positive
4. worry all the time
5. easily distracted
6. generally okay
7. balanced meals
8. emotionally tired

Dictation

1. My grandmother is a (mature) (eighty) years old.
2. She's (energetic) but (forgetful).
3. The (elderly) are sometimes (frustrated).
4. They can't be as (active) as they once were.
5. I feel (guilty) for not spending more time with her.
6. I'm usually (exhausted) by the end of the day.

 Dictation

1. energy drink
2. new dentures
3. total frustration
4. think actively
5. guilt-ridden
6. seventy-eight years old
7. ninety-four
8. eighty-two

unit 19 • **writings** • Lists

 Dictation

1. I have great (expectations) for next year!
2. No more (excuses)!
3. If you get up (earlier), you can (exercise).
4. He has to have a (friendlier) (attitude).
5. I need to (improve) my diet.
6. I want to stop (watching) so much TV.
7. (Choose) your friends carefully.

 Dictation

1. new and improved
2. user-friendly
3. exercise bike
4. probable cause
5. New Year's resolutions
6. exception to the rule
7. negative thinking
8. stamp out negativity

unit 20 • **writings** • Dear Diary

 The **ed** ending on past tense verbs has three pronunciations. Compare **decided**, **finished** and **believed**. If the base word ends with the sounds **t** or **d** (**expect** / **decide**), the **ed** sounds like **id**. If the base word ends in a "soft" sound (**finish**, **laugh**, **escape**), the **ed** sounds like **t**. If the base word ends in a vowel sound (**follow**, **try**, **pray**), a "hard" sound (**remember**, **realize**, **believe**) or a nasal sound (**learn**, **dream**, **smell**), the **ed** sounds like **d**.

This **ed** pattern holds true for adjectives. Compare **excited**, **flushed**, and **bored**.

 Dictation

1. I (followed) my heart.
2. I (remembered) his birthday too late, so I (decided) to ignore it.
3. I (realized) too late that I had (believed) the wrong person.
4. They (laughed) when I said I've always (dreamed) of a big wedding.
5. I (learned) my lesson the hard way.
6. We (finished) my birthday cake in record time.

 Dictation

1. danced all night
2. recaptured the romance
3. candles melted
4. bit and scratched
5. botched up the job
6. realized too late
7. wrecked the party
8. rummaged around

Dictation

1. The (clinic) opens at 10 a.m.
2. The (doctor's) (payment) is (due) tomorrow.
3. My usual (babysitter) is on (holidays).
4. Our tenth (anniversary) is next month.
5. My kid's (graduation) was yesterday.
6. Her baseball (practice) starts at 6 p.m.

 Dictation

1. doctor's appointment at 8:30 a.m.
2. baseball tournament begins
3. garbage pickup*
4. Sam's birthday
5. return video by 1 p.m.
6. rent due
7. vacation starts
8. check out* apartment

 pickup* / check out*: **Pickup** is one word because it is a noun. **Check out** is two words because it is a verb. This noun/verb pattern applies in all cases. Other examples include **shutdown / shut down** ; **workout / work out** ; **breakup / break up**.

 June (end of school / start of baseball season).

Spelling Rules

The Doubling rule

If a word has one syllable and ends with one vowel and one consonant, double the final consonant when you add an end part that starts with a vowel.

Note: *x* and *w* are never doubled.

The Y rule: Part 1

When you hear the long *e* sound at the end of a word that has two or more syllables, use *y*.

The Y rule: Part 2

If a word ends in consonant + *y*, the *y* changes to *i* when you add all end parts, except *ing*.

Silent E rule

When you add the letter *e* to the end of a word, the short vowel sound in that word changes to a long vowel sound.

Drop the E rule

If a word ends with a silent *e*, drop the silent *e* before you add an end part that starts with a vowel.

Spelling Patterns in Alphabetical Order

able ible

ack eck ick ock uck

adge edge idge odge udge

age

al

ance ence

ant ent

ary

atch etch itch otch utch

ble cle dle kle ple

ic

ity

ive

ment

ous

sion tion

ture

Spelling Patterns in Each Unit

Unit 1: **tion** (as in **action**)

Unit 2: **ture** (as in **adventure**) / **ous** (as in **hilarious**)

Unit 3: **tion** (as in **congratulations**) / **ic** (as in **fantastic**) / **ity** (as in **hospitality**)

Unit 4: short vowel + **tch** (as in **catch**, **fetch**, **itch**, etc.) / **age** (as in **garbage**)

Unit 5: Review of spelling patterns

Unit 6: **ance**, **ence** / **dge** (as in **badge**, **edge**, **fridge**, etc.)

Unit 7: Review of spelling patterns

Unit 8: short vowel + **ck** (as in **stack**, **check**, **stick**, **block**, **stuck**) / **sion** (as in **decision**)

Unit 9: **ive** (as in **positive**) / **al** (as in **general**)

Unit 10: Review of spelling patterns

Unit 11: **ent**, **ant** / **ible**, **able**

Unit 12: **ary** (as in **ordinary**) / **ment** (as in **appointment**)

Unit 13: Review of spelling patterns

Unit 14: Review of spelling patterns

Unit 15: consonant + **le** (as in **trouble**, **handle**, **simple**)

Unit 16: Review of spelling patterns

Unit 17: Review of spelling patterns

Unit 18: Review of spelling patterns

Unit 19: Review of spelling patterns

Unit 20: Review of spelling patterns

Unit 21: Review of spelling patterns